A BEGINNER'S GUIDE TO GETTING PUBLISHED

A BEGINNER'S GUIDE TO GETTING PUBLISHED

Edited by
Kirk Polking

Writer's Digest Books
Cincinnati, Ohio

Library of Congress Cataloging-in-Publication Data

A. beginner's guide to getting published.
  Includes index.
  1. Authorship—Marketing. I. Polking, Kirk.
PN161.B44 1987   808'.02   87-6176
ISBN 0-89879-260-6

The following two pages are an extension of this copyright page.

Acknowledgments

Some of the articles in this book appeared originally in either *Writer's Digest,* *Writer's Yearbook,* or one of the *Writer's Digest Guides.* Some articles are reprinted from other sources as indicated. In each case, the chapters are revised and updated and reprinted by permission of the author.

Rose Adkins, "Creatively Marketing Your Manuscripts," copyright © 1982 *Christian Writer.*

Ludmilla Alexander, "You're Never Too Young to Be a Published Writer," copyright © 1981, *Writer's Digest.*

Donna Anders, "Writing the Juvenile Mystery," copyright © 1982, *WDS Forum,* Writer's Digest School.

Louise Boggess, "Easy First Sales: Fillers," copyright © 1979 *WDS Forum,* Writer's Digest School.

Jean Bryant, "The Seven Laws of Writing," excerpted from *Anybody Can Write* by Jean Bryant. Copyright © 1986 by Jean Bryant. Reprinted by permission of Whatever Publishing, Inc., San Rafael, California.

James Dulley, "How to Self-Syndicate Your Newspaper Column," *1986 Writer's Yearbook,* copyright © 1986 Writer's Digest Publications.

Scott Edelstein, "A Writer's Guide to Income Taxes," excerpted from *The Indispensable Writer's Guide,* copyright © 1987 by Scott Edelstein, reprinted by permission of Harper and Row, Publishers, Inc. An earlier and less comprehensive version of this article originally appeared in the January 1985 *Writer's Digest* and is copyright 1984 by Writer's Digest. This version has been updated and considerably expanded.

Patricia Ann Emme, "How to Write and Sell Greeting Cards," copyright © 1980, *Writer's Digest.*

John D. Engle, Jr., "A Primer for Poets," copyright © 1983, *Writer's Digest.*

Dennis E. Hensley, "A Treasurehouse in Trade Journals," copyright © 1981, *Writer's Digest.*

Helen Hinckley Jones, "Writing the Story of Accomplishment," copyright © 1980, *WDS Forum,* Writer's Digest School.

Judy Keene, "Turning Local into National Magazine Article Sales," copyright © 1984, *WDS Forum,* Writer's Digest School.

Leonard L. Knott, "How to Enjoy Books, Theater and the Movies—for Free!" excerpted from *Writing After Fifty,* copyright © 1985, by Leonard L. Knott, published by Writer's Digest Books.

Mansfield Latimer, "Are There Hidden Sales In Your Files?" copyright © 1982, *Writer's Digest.*

Don McKinney, "How to Write True-Life Dramas," copyright © 1986,

Contents

Preface

What are the best break-in points to seeing your name in print? There are hundreds of choices, but they can be grouped into two primary categories, as follows: (1) publishing outlets whose payment is a byline and personal satisfaction in doing creative work that is appreciated; and (2) less well-known but "easier" and less competitive markets willing to pay for and publish fillers, poetry, gags, greeting card verse, plus short stories and articles.

This book is divided into three sections. The first section offers opportunities to gain recognition as a writer; the second section shows the way to move up the professional ladder; and the final section provides reminders on some important details about freelancing as a business.

In the first section, you'll see that you can gain recognition with a byline, no matter what age you begin. Also you will find, as part of your apprenticeship to getting published, that there are gifts only you as a writer can give. Remember too, that letters to the editors of newspapers and magazines can be just the springboard you need to publication, plus they can help you develop your skills in making a point effectively while using as few words as possible. Such published letters will bring your name to the attention of editors, who will see that you read their publications thoroughly and understand their readers. Weekly newspapers generally have very small staffs and are usually looking for correspondents to cover areas of the county they can't reach regularly. Large metropolitan dailies welcome literate commentaries on local and national news for their editorial-page letters column.

Your community can also help you develop your writing experience. Does your church need an editor for its weekly bulletin? Does the PTA need a newsletter to help improve relations between school and parents? Does the local Heart Association, Cancer Society, or Children's Hospital need someone to help with fund-raising brochures or a publication to unify its volunteer groups? Are you politically minded? Does a local candidate need your help with speeches or campaign literature? Initially, these jobs may pay you only a smile of thanks, but they can lead to financial rewards later.

When you're ready to try broadening your freelance efforts beyond the local area, you'll want to consult the chapters in this book that will show you how to successfully create gag ideas for magazine cartoonists; fillers for magazines; and poems and greeting card verse to other organizations—usually for payment.

There are other methods of moving up professionally. Writers who tend to think of magazine markets as only those they see on the newsstand or in their local library are overlooking hundreds of hidden markets that we describe in this book—juvenile magazines, religious publications, literary and little magazines whose editors encourage new writers and cater to the broadest spectrum of literary, social, and political taste imaginable in the stories and articles they buy.

Keep in mind, however, that some of the markets mentioned in this book as examples may move, or change their editorial slant, or go out of business only to be replaced by newer publications. So be sure to check the latest directories such as *Writer's Market*, *Fiction Writer's Market*, and *The International Directory of Little Magazines and Small Presses* for their most recent editorial requirements.

If there is a good opportunity for beginning writers not mentioned in this book that you've uncovered and would like to share with others, drop me a line so that, in planning for the next edition, we can consider an article on that subject, with *you* as its author!

Kirk Polking

SECTION ONE: GAINING RECOGNITION AS A WRITER

How to Break into Your Local Weekly Newspaper

Bim Angst

Editors at the 6,811 weekly newspapers in this country are crying, literally, for good local features. I know. I'm one of them, and I wail each week when I scan the personal announcements and club news sent in by my fifteen correspondents. In their own neighborhoods are stories I'd love to publish, but I don't have the time to write them myself, and I can't afford the time to train a staff writer to get the stories for me. At night I dream of discovering six freelance writers who could supply me with the local features I need every week. But I'd be satisfied with one writer who could give me six features.

I have a file cabinet full of feature ideas that I'd love to pass on to someone else. But first I want to know that person is capable of recognizing feature possibilities. If you've got the notion that everything has feature possibilities, move to central, eastern Pennsylvania and give me a call—fast.

Developing the idea for a feature isn't nearly as easy as finding an idea. Sure, I'd love to know about the new road signs the neighboring borough of Nesquehoning just put up, but a business profile of a sign factory in Wisconsin isn't going to interest my readers. However, the story, using the words of the designer, of how he studied the topography of the town and used his impressions to design the signs—well, for that story I'd give you the run of my own office, complete with phone and typewriter, for a whole afternoon. I'd even let you borrow a photographer.

The key is local interest. I don't care what the Canadians are doing about noisy geese—unless the local town of Tamaqua is trying out the method. I don't want to read about heart transplants—unless a lady who grew up in nearby Albrightsville is recovering from one. My readers aren't concerned with the high cost of living nationwide: they want to know what ground beef costs in Lehighton. We may feel compassion for the plight of farmers in Iowa, but here we need to know who will lose his job if a farm in West Penn Township goes under.

Every story has a local angle. That's why the weekly newspaper exists. Big-city dailies give us all the news we want about the world, the nation, even our home states. But we want to know about our neighbors, too, and the weekly newspaper is trying to satisfy that desire. The feature story is the weekly's stock-in-trade. The dailies inevitably beat it to fast-breaking news, but because the staff of a daily is geared toward what happened today, the stories that take time to unfold are often overlooked. Because there are so many car accidents, drug busts, council meetings, sports scores, and murder trials to report, the daily newspaper cannot hope to cover the birthday parties for ladies turning 100 at Weatherwood (the Carbon County Home for the Aged), the efforts of the Little Schuylkill Conservation Club, or the effects of the burgeoning tourist industry on the life-long residents of Old Mauch Chunk. The weekly covers all these stories precisely because it cannot compete with the daily for fast-breaking news.

Because he's not concerned with putting out another issue in sixteen hours, the editor of a weekly newspaper may have more time to talk to you than will the editor of a daily. Get to him on the day his paper comes out. All his work was complete the day before, and he's searching hard now for people to write the features he wants to run next week. Give him a call and ask to come see him. Don't tell him you are a freelance writer. (Editors at weekly newspapers have a fear of freelancers. They think freelancers are prima donnas who insist on complete editorial control over their work and demand hundreds of dollars for each article.) Tell him you have some ideas for features and you'd like to write them for his paper. When he tells you he can't pay much, bite your tongue and tell him you understand. Then forget about money for a bit and go sell him your ideas.

Editors at weekly newspapers are often also sales reps for the advertising their papers carry, so keep your pitch as direct and brief as his would be. The editor just wants to know enough to feel confident that you can write the story you say you can. If you've got published clips of newspaper features you've written, take them for him to peruse. If you don't have clips, don't panic. Type a brief list of questions for each of your article ideas and let him look at those.

Here's an example: Suppose your neighbor belongs to a pistol club, the Women's Pistol Club, which has a target range in Aquashicola. The club's been active for years; members have even taken championships. The sports editors of the dailies cover events and results, but no one has ever featured the women sharpshooters. Your article suggestion might look like this:

Women's Pistol Club

Why do members join?

How do their boyfriends, parents, husbands, and kids handle having them shoot pistols?

Do they feel they're encouraging violence?

What do they get out of shooting?

Does their size and strength affect their shooting style?

How do they rate against men shooters?

Do they face bias from judges and audiences? If so, how do they handle it?

It's a lot more than finding out who the coach is and how many members there are, although that background information is necessary and useful.

Here's another possibility for an article: The Chief of Obstetrics at Coaldale Hospital is retiring. Every paper will do a feature on the man, but yours will stand out—and has to because it's in a weekly and will probably hit the streets later than the stories in the dailies—if you focus it differently. Of course, you'll have to ask how many babies he's brought into the world. But then go further. Speak to several women whose children he delivered. Find a family where he delivered a daughter and then the grandchild. The family angle and contrast of birthing styles may be very interesting. It will be just as interesting if there is no difference in birthing styles over twenty to forty years. Did he deliver his own children? If not, why not? How do the nurses feel about working with him? Has he delivered any of their children? Speak to his wife and family and find out the joys and trials his profession has placed on them. If he delivered your kids, you've got a very special story in the works already.

Ask the right questions and your editor can make the answers into a feature. If you can't ask the right questions, it won't matter how nicely you craft a sentence. When the editor says he'll look at your article but he can't promise you anything, consider yourself in like Flynn.

But don't leave his office yet. Go over your list of questions with him. Ask his advice. Is this problem of houses and trees slipping down into abandoned mines, what's called *mine subsidence*, important to the people who live near the quarries in Palmerton? The editor will be glad to tell you how to get to the quarry so you can talk to the people who live near it. Would it be wise to get the County Planning Director to comment on the problem county-wide? Would a contractor be able to provide information on how it influences new building? The editor will be glad to give you phone numbers.

Call the people he mentions. Mention to them that he told you to call. They may be more willing to talk to you, and more informative, if they know you're working for a newspaper editor. Use your editor's suggestions as a guide for your research.

Okay, so now you've spoken to everybody you can get to in the time before your article has to be on the editor's desk. (Ask the editor what his deadline is for the upcoming issue. Don't make him wait for your story. He might forget you, or worse, might remember you're late with your piece.) Now you have to shape the information into something people will enjoy reading. People read features for pleasure. Use any method you can to organize your story into something that's pleasant to read. If you've got a good lead, the pieces of your research will fall together almost by themselves. Quotes convey the personalities of your sources and their attitudes on your topic. A light touch will keep the reader reading.

To tailor your article to the interests of the newspaper, read the features they've printed recently. How are they focused? Who are they aimed at? What are the interests of the readers? The more detailed a picture of the readers you get, the more pleasurable the article is. Play detective. Writing for your audience means a lot more than knowing that the reader lives in Summit Hill.

When you get through the first draft of your feature, it will be at least three times longer than it should be. It should be just long enough to tell the story but short enough to ensure that the editor will use it no matter how tight his paper is the night it gets pasted up. Brevity is your ticket to getting published. Editors are realists, especially when confronted with a page that has only twenty column-inches for text. Take out your flowing prose, and ax the extraneous background information. Get down to a single focus. (The background you dug up was necessary: you can't recognize a good lead or strong focus if you don't have the whole picture first.)

Then think about where your newspaper is read. It will be read in spurts—while the potatoes are boiling, while the kids are in the tub, while the reader is waiting for the carpool driver to show up. If the reader scans and finds an article too long, he'll skip it. The editor will get no good comments on it, and he won't want to see another article from you next week.

After you've custom-fit your article, the editor will refit it, sometimes brutally. He'll cut whole paragraphs, rearrange points, alter headlines, and reduce your prose. This is his prerogative. Remember who's paying you.

You probably won't get paid for your article before it's published. My newspaper, *MidWeeker*, pays 10¢ a double-column line, about 1¢ to 1½¢ a word. That isn't much when you think about the time you put into the article. But you'll get more efficient. Console yourself for now with the knowledge that you'll use the clippings of that newspaper feature to get assignments at regional and national magazines. The feature may have provided you with the basic research for an expanded article on the same topic. That dinky feature proves you're capable of asking the right questions and focusing and shaping the answers, and that you can handle even the most drastic editing. (Even big-time editors don't want to deal with prima donnas.)

As you move on to the big time, don't forget about your weekly newspaper editor. He pays your mileage and postage. Show him you can write consistently and that you've learned quickly, and he'll start talking per-assignment rather than per-line fees. Prove to him that you can deliver what he needs when he needs it, and he'll consider giving you a press card and making you a staff writer. Show initiative and assertiveness, and he'll make you assistant editor. I would.

Easy First Sales: Fillers

Louise Boggess

At a luncheon, the woman sitting beside me pointed to her overweight friend at the end of the table and remarked, "She bought a reducing machine last week for a ridiculous price."

The comment kept cropping up in my mind all during the luncheon as a possible filler. Before I arrived home several hours later, I had written in my notebook: "Substitute *figure* for *price* so statement reads, 'She bought a reducing machine last week for a ridiculous figure.' " The slight change made a salable filler.

Filler refers to a short item used to enliven the pages of a magazine. It may vary from a beautifully turned phrase to a personal experience of five-hundred words. Originally, the filler completed an unfinished page, but today, magazines use them to make up special sections under titles many readers recognize, such as "Life in These United States" from *Reader's Digest*.

Fillers and short features offer anyone an exceptional opportunity to write and sell. You can write and sell because the editor buys the material regardless of who wrote it—a known or an unknown writer. Also, writing fillers requires very little time. In fact, you simply work on the margins of time by jotting down items while you wait in the dentist's office or eat your lunch.

TRAVEL ALERT

Amazingly, you can earn from one hundred to three hundred dollars a month by selling these short items. Furthermore, think of the satisfaction you derive from sharing some special knowledge, a bit of laughter, an interesting personality, or a dramatic experience with thousands of people.

Writing fillers also appeals to the professional writer, but in a different way. In doing research for writing fiction or nonfiction, he comes across items that will sell as fillers. The money from these fillers helps with the cost of research. While he does not go looking for them, he rarely misses any, more or less, handed to him. But writing fillers offers him only a sideline.

On the other hand, the beginner must learn where to look for filler ideas. In a very short time, he discovers fillers all around him. Think of fillers and short features as brief playbacks from life. To find these playbacks, become aware of what people do, say, or think. The more you socialize with people, the more ideas you find. So begin your search for filler ideas by observing the world around you.

An alertness when traveling pays dividends. Look for humorous signs on marquees, in front of stores, in store windows, on panel trucks, or on billboards. Small towns offer very fertile ground for this type of lookout. A sign on the highway said: "You Came You Saw Utah."

This sign appeared on a car-wash place: "Have Soap Will Wash." A carpet store advertised: "Our Prices Will Floor You." A car-body shop carried this one: "Scrap Metal for Sick Cars."

Signs appear in places you least expect. During a heavy California rain, the drainage systems overflowed and water reached the doorways of many houses in a tract. One owner promptly put up this homemade sign: "For Sale Cheap This Lakeside Property." This resulted in a quick filler sale.

Actions of people, like words, make good fillers. Never wait idly in an airport or any place crowded with people, but study the actions and reactions of people. You may find a filler.

A young mother between planes at the airport handed her youngster a plastic sack filled with building blocks. He dumped the blocks made of colored sponges on the floor without a sound. This suggested an excellent hint for traveling with youngsters.

Emotional actions of people make good filler material. In an adult-education class for the foreign born, the teacher asked each person to either sing or recite his national anthem as a means of getting acquainted with each other. When the turn of a Hungarian refugee came, he refused to sing the song of his country but proudly burst into "God Bless America."

Your power of observation can lead you to other fillers. Watch for unusual hobbies of your friends and acquaintances. Notice outstanding window displays in stores. Take a picture and interview the person in charge so you can write a short explanation. Businesspersons use time-saving or labor-saving shortcuts in all types of work. Look for them. A sale awaits you at the appropriate business publication.

Observation offers only one means of finding filler and short feature material. You must also learn to listen.

No one needs a license to listen, but you can profit from what you hear.

When a proud parent wants to tell you about the bright sayings of her child, listen. If a friend relates a funny sight she saw at a bus station, get every detail. Ask questions if necessary. By adding a few words here and there, you have possibly a salable anecdote.

Tune in on the conversations of others while you wait in a crowd. Two secretaries discussed another person while waiting in the luncheon line. "She uses all the brains she has," one said. The other quipped, "And all she can borrow." A woman in the theater line explained to her friend how she mended the finger of her glove by using a lipstick as a darning egg.

Family and college reunions provide good listening for filler ideas. Everyone has sharpened his memory. You hear old sayings, puns, or humorous incidents. Take along a tape recorder so that you can gather all the information. Later, you can run the tape at your leisure and check for filler material.

Many people earn a living by speaking with a humorous tongue. Listen with fillers in mind when you hear a lecturer, a luncheon speaker, a disc jockey, or a stand-up comic. Don't overlook television, radio, and comic records as excellent means of fillers. (Short jokes and gags are uncopyrightable, but a long, humorous monologue could not be reused without permission.)

The trouble with listening is that you don't want to stop to write. But you need not depend on crowds exclusively, for you can find ideas even when you read.

Read Everything

Always read with pen and pad available. Biographies offer odd and intimate glimpses of famous people. Short stories, articles, and books represent the author's best words. All suggest sources of well-turned phrases, clever puns, or humorous statements. Poetry provides excellent imagery and figures of speech that will sell as fillers.

Most editors accept a short, direct quotation—say, up to one hundred words from a copyrighted full-length book, article, or short story—as not infringing on the copyright as long as you cite the source. You couldn't, however, quote, for example, a single line from a very short poem or song without getting the author's permission. For such a situation or a longer quotation from copyrighted material, you would write the publisher for permission. Some magazines that use fillers pay the originator as well as the one who submits the filler.

Books of quotations stimulate your mind to think in epigrams and quips. Often, a statement made in early Greece applies to today. Form the habit of buying books—many are available in paperback—of humorous, well-known, and popular quotations. The cost proves nominal when compared to what you can earn selling epigrams and quips.

If you intend to write fillers, study the magazines you wish to sell. Often, one filler will free your subconscious to remember a similar incident. You have heard the old expression, "That's not the way I heard it." Often in reading fillers, you see the possibility of an entirely different one for another market.

Take, for instance, the book title *Happiness Is a Warm Puppy*. You can define happiness in any number of ways: Happiness means learning your neighbor's boy no longer serves as Scout bugler. Try some spinoffs yourself on defining happiness.

Newsletters and in-service publications of organizations often contain filler material. From one newsletter came this unusual fact: "The world's only international streetcar line runs between El Paso, Texas, and Ciudad Juarez, Chihuahua, Mexico."

Read annual reports for historical facts, new scientific research, or new products. You may sell a scientific or unusual fact, a new use for an old product, or information on a new one. Other similar sources of fillers include sales and promotion letters, envelope stuffers, and advertisements.

Study your newspaper for funny typographical errors. *Reader's Digest* printed this one from a Kentucky newspaper's society report on a New Year's Eve party: "The large room was vividly decorated with red noses." Headlines may appear funny, too. Take this one published in the magazine of the Brazil *Herald*: "Birth Control Bears Fruit."

SHORT STUFF

Regular news stories relate antics of animals, odd coincidences in unrelated events, and happenings in the lives of well-known people. Some paragraphs from the newspapers lend themselves to humorous comment, as appears in *The New Yorker* filler. You may use any news material from a newspaper, since news, like facts, is uncopyrightable. Signed feature articles and syndicated columns, however, are copyrighted, and only brief excerpts could be used (with credit to the writer or columnist) under the fair-use provision of the copyright law.

So, make any reading you do pay dividends in money as well as pleasure.

Consider your own experience the primary source of all filler material. Some editors like first-person experiences because they provide one-to-one contact with the reader.

For example, train yourself to look for fillers as you clean house, sew, or cook. If you think of ways to entertain your children or to work out an agreeable solution to a family problem, you may likely have filler material. Always make notations immediately on children's funny sayings, before you forget them.

In addition, look around your office for shortcuts to better business. If you have a home shop, look for better ways of handling a task there. Farmers, seek shortcuts to better farming.

More and more magazines have added fillers and short features. To expand your sales, get acquainted with *Writer's Market*, which lists many magazines that buy fillers and short features. You can locate this information easily by the specific subhead, "fillers," under each listing.

When you become more experienced in searching for material, you will develop a built-in antenna that alerts you constantly to filler material.

You're Never Too Young to Be a Published Writer

Ludmilla Alexander

You may not be old enough to own a driver's license, or vote in an election, or even to have gone on a first date. But you are definitely old enough to be a published author.

Age is no factor in receiving a byline. Ability is. Editors from all over the United States have purchased articles, poems, and stories from youngsters sixteen years old and under.

Impossible, you say, after seeing your highly praised story rejected nine times. Then ask Cynthia Hanson of Maple Glen, Pennsylvania. Cynthia began writing for *Seventeen Magazine* when she was fifteen. She had been reading the magazine since age twelve and believed she could write as well as any of the authors that were being published. She submitted an article about her vacation with her friends. *Seventeen* bought it. She then submitted book reviews, an article on learning to drive, and a gift-ideas guide—all were accepted.

Sound easy? It's not always so. Karen Frayne of San Jose, California, had been writing since the first grade. She won poetry and speech-writing contests. Her teachers were amazed at her imagination and skill in writing. When she was in the seventh grade, she decided to try publishing her work. "I would get letters from editors praising my work, yet no sales," she said. "Some editors would jot, 'I hope you keep writing.' Based on this encouragement, I did keep writing. I ignored the rejection slips, figuring that I just got started."

Finally, Karen began making headway. One of her poems was published in the Dynamite section of the *San Jose Mercury News*. Then, a 270-word, true-life experience was printed in the National Zoo Magazine's section for children. That piece brought her $27.50.

Cheryl Dragel, of Downers Grove, Illinois, has also fought an uphill battle. She sent in two poems to *Seventeen* and one was accepted. Success! But then, Cheryl sent in forty more poems and *all* were rejected. Did she give up? No. "I was determined to succeed," she said. "I felt that if I sold one poem then why not another? And if I didn't keep on submitting them, I would never know if I could ever succeed."

Finally, "Rain Dance" was published, and Cheryl began expanding her markets. *Teen Magazine, Hanging Loose, Encore Magazine*, and *Southwest* literary magazine all accepted her work. When her family visited Cape Cod she wrote about their experiences. Her article was published in the *Cape Cod Times*.

JUST FOR KIDS

When writing for *Cape Cod Times* and *Southwest*, Cheryl had to compete with adult writers for the editors' attention. And it's true that most juvenile and young-adult magazines are written by adult freelancers with many years of experience in the field. If you look closely at magazines and newspapers that are in your home, however, you will find that many have special sections for young writers.

Other magazines, such as *Stone Soup*, actually *need* manuscripts from young authors. *Stone Soup* publishes fiction, poems, songs, and drawings exclusively by children thirteen years of age and under.

What should you write about? Good question! Writers of all ages have been battling with this question for centuries. It's too simple to say, "Write what you know." Hundreds of manuscripts about vacations cross editors' desks, for instance. The subject has been written to death—and yet, Cynthia Hanson's article about traveling with friends was published. And so was Cheryl Dragel's, on her experiences on Cape Cod with her family.

What made the difference?

"I wait until I experience something before I write about it," explained Cynthia Hanson. "A long time ago, a title popped into my head about being a lifeguard. Yet, I didn't start writing the article until I experienced being a lifeguard last summer."

"We seldom receive hackneyed stories about the death of pets," said William Rubel, coeditor of *Stone Soup*. "The subject moves the young authors, and they write deeply about the death or the loss of their pet."

Rubel suggests keeping a notebook for writing—as an artist keeps a sketch pad. Authors should formulate ideas—what types of color they like and why. What they think of the morning lights, the light at dusk. What do their friends like? How do people treat one another?

Here are some more tips and rules from editors that will help you be a better—and perhaps a published—writer.

One: Get those nouns and verbs tucked firmly in your brain.

Editors complain again and again about the poor grammar in manuscripts.

"Often grammar is so bad that it takes too much time to correct the manuscript," said one. Another added, "Long, wordy stories with no angle, little thought, and hardly any attention to writing style are rejected."

Two: Go for the unique.

Editors, it seems, receive the same old stuff again and again. "Most articles are rejected just because they're too common or too normal to be interesting to our readers," said a *Tiger Beat* editor.

William Rubel of *Stone Soup* added, "The most common problem of rejected manuscripts is formula writing. Martians are always green. Aliens always destroy the world. Poets always concentrate on winter, spring, and Easter."

How many times have you read about a dog that saves a family from a fire? Or a boy who plays sports poorly, but makes the winning point in a championship game? Or a girl who loses her boyfriend to a beautiful but sneaky classmate, then wins him back because she is sweet, kind, and honest?

Other topics editors don't want to see are jogging, babysitting techniques, and pet care.

They don't want to see such manuscripts unless—and this is a big *unless*—you can come up with something unique about the subject. Perhaps there is a twist in the plot, and the dog, after saving the family, discovers who set fire to the house. Or, perhaps the babysitting techniques are given by a teenager who has set up a business with all her friends, and they donate portions of their earnings to the company for advertising, training, and self-protection measures. Then the editors may just sit up and take notice.

On the other hand, you can turn even common subjects and plots into works of art with strong writing.

For example, rain. Common. Nothing exciting. But if you write imaginatively, as Cheryl Dragel did in an issue of *Seventeen*, rain takes on a completely new dimension. Here's what she wrote:

> Gingerbread people, who melt when they get wet,
> take refuge under awnings and umbrellas
> as the first droplets of rain hit the pavement.

I run out (minus umbrella) in bare feet
splashing in a newborn puddle
to watch raindrops dancing
on a once grimy street.

Three: Find a gentle critic.

People who read a lot know instinctively whether a manuscript is good or not. These people can tell you if the manuscript is ready to make the rounds or if it needs more work.

Find such a critic. He may be a parent, a teacher, an older brother or sister, or even a friend. Take your critic's advice cheerfully, and follow it.

Be careful that your critics don't start rewriting your manuscript to suit their standards, however. "We reject material that leaves us with the suspicion that the author had a lot of parent help on the piece," said one editor.

"Too much encouragement can be discouraging," added William Rubel. "After all, not everything is good. Children are realistic and can appraise their own work. Parents should be supportive, but not make a big production."

Four: Be persistent.

"Teenagers who have made it with *Seventeen* have been persistent writers," said one fiction/teen features editor. "They started with a few prose pieces and poems, and kept on submitting. Then they went on to longer pieces. Finally, we turned to them and assigned material such as book reviews."

Anne Irwin, of Whitefish Bay, Wisconsin, reached the envied status of having a *Seventeen* editor call *her*. With her first article, she included a cover letter, telling what she did in school, her activities, and the fact that she was in the Gifted Student Writers' Program. The editors rejected the article but liked her style. They asked her to write about teen writing; her work was published in the Frankly Speaking column.

She then wrote about a trip to Austria with the school band and orchestra. After accepting the story, the editors contacted her to write an article about Shakespeare. *Seventeen* also sends her a list of articles that they are looking for.

Five: Develop a thick skin.

Rejections hurt, whether you are thirteen and have been writing for a year, or forty-three and have been writing for twenty. When that rejection slip appears in the mailbox, don't think, "I'm no good," but rather, "My manuscript didn't fit in."

"There are many reasons for rejection," said one editor. "Very possibly, something similar was used recently."

"You can't worry whether your work is rejected or accepted," advised Reid Ackley from Franconia, New Hampshire. "I sold three poems to *Seventeen*, and now I hesitate to try again. And yet, if I did it once, I should be able to do it again."

"My advice is to believe in yourself and keep trying," added Cheryl Dragel. "You'll never know until you try."

Finally, should you tell the editor your age? That is probably the most common question asked by young writers. Many editors don't want to know your age. They are interested in high-quality material regardless of the author's age. Period.

So, don't envy that nineteen-year-old just because he can drive a car and you can't. Believe me, getting a driver's license isn't nearly as exciting as getting a published byline.

CHILDREN'S EXPRESS: A SYNDICATED NEWSPAPER COLUMN

Children's Express (C.E.) is a private, nonprofit news service reported by children who are thirteen years old and under. The reporters work in teams led by children who are fourteen- to eighteen-year-old assistant editors. The twice-weekly C.E. column is carried over the regular UPI wires and distributed to 2,500 newspapers worldwide.

Young authors may write for more information to Children's Express, 20 Charles Street, New York, NY 10014.

C.E. has seven news bureaus in the United States and overseas. The C.E. column has appeared in many major American newspapers, including the *New York Times, New York Daily News, Chicago Sun-Times, Cleveland Plain Dealer, Miami Herald*, and *San Francisco Examiner*. In Japan alone, the column has a regular circulation of 9.4 million through its sponsor, Yomiuri Shimbun. Other bureaus are located in Melbourne, Australia; Wellington, New Zealand; San Francisco Bay Area; Northeast Massachusetts; Newark, New Jersey; and New York City.

How C.E. Works

Over the years, Children's Express has developed and refined training methodology and a system of oral journalism that enables children from a wide variety of backgrounds to participate in its activities. C.E. columns consist of interviews with description and commentary by C.E. reporters or "roundtable" dialogue among reporters or other children the same age.

Reporters, who are thirteen years old and younger, are responsible for asking all questions and providing all dialogue, description, analysis, and opinion in C.E. journalism. The young reporters are backed up and supported by teen editors and a small adult staff.

Teen editors are responsible for all C.E. News Team leadership, management, briefing, and debriefing, as well as for all training, logistics, and research. They choose or review all story ideas, and when possible, they do edits or preliminary edits.

Adults are responsible for business management, final edit, and story assignment. Their most important job is to make sure that reporters and teen editors get all the responsibility they want and can handle.

History

C.E. first gained wide public attention when it scooped the world press on Carter's choice of Mondale at the Democratic National Convention in 1976. Since then, C.E. has produced almost two thousand articles, a book, and magazine reports for *Rolling Stone, Family Circle,* and *Elle,* and a series of TV reports for *Today.* Its reporters have held four sets of widely covered hearings on children's issues, and its news teams have traveled to the refugee camps on the Thailand-Cambodian border, to Hiroshima, Tokyo, and the Soviet Union.

The Poet's Primer

John D. Engle Jr.

The extent of your success in writing and publishing poetry depends largely on your attitude toward yourself and your writing. It also depends on your attitude toward learning and applying the answers to the following questions: *1. What is poetry? 2. How do I know when I've written a good poem? 3. What is the poetry market? How do I prepare to enter it? 4. What are the different kinds of poetry outlets? Where do I find them? How do I plug into them?* I hope to answer some of these questions and help you to start off with a realistic attitude so that your road to publication will be easier to travel.

BECOMING A POET, IN EVERY SENSE OF THE WORD

Your attitude is the most significant determinant of your success. It is the net with which you fish the sea of poetry. If the net is faulty, your chances of success will be seriously limited. In general, your attitude toward yourself and your writing should be positive. You must believe in yourself and your ability, and you should feel that you have something important to say and that you have a right to be heard. You are unique. You should recognize, develop, and celebrate your uniqueness and sing life as you see it.

However, there is a danger in carrying this attitude too far. In spite of all the evidence to the contrary, the myth persists that poets are somehow more talented, more divinely inspired, and far wiser than other people. If you believe this, you may ignore basic preparation, rules, and procedures; you may have an exaggerated sense of your importance and the importance of what you write. In other words, your attitude may be unrealistic.

One of the most unrealistic attitudes fathered by the superior-poet myth is the assumption that something called *poetic license,* no doubt invented by someone too lazy to look up misspelled words and learn the rules of grammar, gives the poet rights denied to other creatures. Even a poet would never expect to ride a bicycle, drive a car, or play a piano well without practical instruction and practice; but he somehow feels capable of dashing off a perfect poem with no preparation and with hardly any effort.

Actually, the basic requirements for writing and publishing poetry are rather prosaic but necessary nevertheless. Let's examine these requirements by first trying to learn what poetry is, then establishing criteria that will help us determine when we have written a good poem.

Many insist that if it doesn't rhyme, it's not poetry; others, including some editors, believe that a modern poem that rhymes is too outdated to be a poem.

In view of these conflicts, how can you make an accurate evaluation of your poetry or the poetry of others? Is there a common ground, an area of agreement, a standard of evaluation to which people of various poetic tastes and preferences can subscribe? I think there is, but you must first face the fact that rhyme and meter, or the lack of either, do not determine what is or is not a good poem; for poetry can't be measured fully on the basis of form, pattern, or technique, even though such attributes are important in both writing and evaluating it.

Your attitude toward poetic form or pattern should be as realistic as your attitude toward shoes. If you were selecting shoes, you would probably examine them carefully and try on many pairs for size, comfort, and style before finally choosing the pair you liked best. Even then, you would not wear the same style, color, or brand the rest of your life. It is more likely that you would have several different styles of shoes for different occasions. This is how you should deal with different styles of poetry also, but you don't need to be bound to any style or styles. If you nurture your inner impulses, there will be times when you will kick off your shoes completely and allow your bare feet to print their own individual, original patterns on beaches of beauty that others have not yet discovered.

Freeing yourself from the restrictions of specific forms and techniques will keep you out of the ruts and will bring you to a better understanding of what poetry is and is not. You will find that form and technique do not make a poem any more than a shoe makes a foot. The foot is the real poem; the shoe is but the form in which the poem is wrapped. If the form doesn't fit, the poem will suffer; and to find what the poem is really like, you have to get past its wrappings.

It is true that there are poems in which form and pattern or typographical arrangement are so much a part of the poem that it is almost impossible to separate the *how* from the *what,* as John Ciardi so clearly shows in *How Does a Poem Mean?* Learning this fact becomes another part of your freedom. But you also learn that mastering techniques of form is not the same as mastering the art of writing poetry—any more than making a shoe is the same as making a foot. For example, it doesn't take you long to discover that a sonnet, one of the most rigid forms of poetry, is filled with some of the greatest *and* some of the *worst* poetry ever written. Anyone of average intelligence may be taught to write a perfectly formed sonnet, but no one can guarantee that that sonnet will contain even one line of good poetry.

GIVING YOUR POEM THE ACID TEST

If form and technique are only secondary criteria for determining what a good poem is, what are the primary criteria? I believe that a reasonably workable test can be based on three fairly simple but very important questions: What does the poem say? How well is it said? Is it worth saying?

What Does the Poem Say?

Of course, the meaning or theme or idea of a poem need not be blared in italics, capitals, and exclamations like the central message of a commercial. Rather, it should communicate metaphorically, symbolically, indirectly. The strength of a poem lies mainly in its metaphorical power and in its ability to imply or suggest rather than state directly; and as indicated before, the *how* of a poem may be a basic part of its *what*. But your poem should communicate *something* to the reader, if not on the first reading, at least on the second or third.

How Well Is It Said?

This question leads to the true test of poetry of whatever kind. In fact, it is a basic critical question that can be applied to all writing. If what the poem says is vague, muddled, garbled, ungrammatical, trite, or is conveyed in pompous, precious, sentimental, commonplace, or obsolete language, the poem has serious faults. It does not say very well what it has to say. More often than not, the problem is grammatical. Beginning poets frequently start at the wrong end of the scale. They attempt to write great poetry before learning the basic elements of grammar—good sentence structure, punctuation, spelling, and word usage.

If a poem is a hodgepodge of sentence fragments, run-on sentences, misused words, misspelled words, overworked adjectives, weak passive verbs, incorrect capitalization and punctuation or none at all; if it has an oversupply of *and*'s and *so*'s and is cluttered with the discarded bones of a dead language, such as *'tis, 'twas, thee, thou, o'er,* and *e'er;* or if it is laced with trite phrases, its message will not be stated very well (even though a reader may be able to figure out the message). I am not suggesting that ungrammatical poems are always bad. I am suggesting that we should first learn the rules, then if we wish we may break them by choice rather than by ignorance.

Is It Worth Saying?

The answer to this question will vary somewhat from poet to poet and from reader to reader. If we were perfectly honest, we could have much more "golden" silence simply by admitting that a large part of what we speak and write is really not worth much. We could all improve our word selections and our methods of presenting them through humble, honest self-evaluation. In doing this, we would find that even truth is no defense in the realm of poetry.

For example, all of us will acknowledge the truth that flowers are beautiful; but since everyone already knows that and agrees, what's the value of saying it *unless* we can say it in a new and beautiful way? What is it worth to be told in a poem that love is lovely, beauty is beautiful, sadness is sad, or death is deadly? Yet thousands of poems and songs do nothing more than that, and thousands of poets write these same poems every day with little variation. As a teacher, editor, critic, and contest judge, I get them by the hundreds—the sad poems and the happy poems. They say it is sad to lose a pet, child, parent, husband, wife, friend, lover; they say that having the love of a pet, child, parent, husband, wife, friend, lover is wonderful; they say that this country is great, nature is grand, God is good, and good is better than evil.

I agree with them all because what they say is true. However, it is not said very well, and although it may be worth saying for the poet and for the person for whom the poem was written, it is usually not worth saying in print for a mass audience. The paradox is that although truth is no defense for poetry, poetry must deal with truth. As Emily Dickinson advised, we must "tell all the truth, but tell it slant," which means we must tell it indirectly, figuratively, metaphorically or symbolically, with imagination, originality, and honesty.

But even if you follow all the rules of good writing and your poem passes the three-question test, even if it is brilliantly original and shows great writing talent or genius, you must also follow the rules of marketing as carefully and realistically as you followed the rules of writing.

MARKETING YOUR POETRY

Many outlets for poetry are already collected and classified for you in various publications, with which you should become familiar and either own or have easy access to. These publications and your other writing materials aren't free, of course, but they are no more expensive than tools needed in other activities, such as photography and golf; besides, when you start selling your poems, all your writing expenses are tax-deductible. The publications containing market listings consist of both periodicals and books. Some or all of them may be found at libraries, bookstores, or newsstands.

Poet's Market is published by Writer's Digest Books, 1507 Dana Avenue, Cincinnati, OH 45207. Also published at the same address are two other guides that are for writers in general, but that contain markets and other helpful material for poets. They are the monthly *Writer's Digest* and the annual *Writer's Yearbook*. *Writer's Digest* runs a regular column on poetry by Judson Jerome, along with up-to-date information about new poetry markets, contests, etc. *Writer's Yearbook* contains many helpful articles and ratings of the top 100 markets.

You should subscribe to *CODA: Poets & Writers Newsletter,* published five times a year by Poets & Writers, Inc., 201 W. 54th Street, New York, NY 10019. This publication is loaded with markets as well as information about publishing, grants, awards, contests, conferences, and many other items of interest to poets.

For an almost endless supply of markets for beginners, you may wish to order the annual *International Directory of Little Magazines and Small Presses,* which contains valuable information about more than 3,000 market listings. It may be ordered from Dustbooks, Box 100, Paradise, CA 95969, or you may be able to find it in your library.

Markets will, no doubt, be duplicated in these various sources; besides, it will take some time to collect them all. Therefore, I suggest you start with *Poet's Market,* which offers a good general introduction to all kinds of poetry outlets. Before going to any one market section, however, I urge you to read all the introductory material and other helps and suggestions; then examine the table of contents and take a slow tour through the book.

Like most beginners, you may protest the low pay of these publications and insist on finding other markets. You are free to do this, of course; but your chances of getting published in big, high-paying magazines are much slimmer because they use less poetry.

The reason most small magazines don't pay much, frequently in copies only, is that they can't afford to. They are usually run by small staffs, many of them unpaid, or by only one or two arts-dedicated people. They carry little or no advertising, and therefore, are lucky to break even financially. However, they provide a valuable proving ground for beginners; and, oddly enough, they frequently publish better poetry than is usually found in larger, commercial, high-paying publications. It is not easy to get published in these small magazines, especially the literary publications. You must be patient and persistent.

BOOKS OF POETRY

Publishing a book of poems may be possible, but isn't likely for a beginner. As for the subsidy publishers, I urge you to steer clear of them unless you have huge amounts of money to invest in a nonprofit venture. Your best bet is to publish first in the magazines then collect your published works into a book and see if you can find a publisher who will take it. If not, you may want to try getting it printed on your own through a local printer.

TRUE SUCCESS AS A POET

The ocean of poetry contains many shallows and depths and endless forms of life and song. You start your adventure by studying the maps and charts of those who have been there before you; then you explore the beaches, harbors, coves, and beyond. But whether you walk, wade, swim, fish, sail, dive, or merely sit and enjoy, you cannot lose. My wish is that you experience as much of that ocean as you feel you must, and my hope is that what I have written here will somehow help you to do it.

Making Puzzles for Profit

William Sunners

I have been constructing and selling original crosswords since before the Depression. My work appears in the newspapers, magazines, and syndicates listed in *Writer's Market*, but I also sell to publications other than the known, crowded, and established ones, and I've sold hundreds of puzzles for $50 to $175 each. These markets are all around you, but like the sleeping princess of the childhood fairy tale, they must be awakened before they can appreciate your constructions.

You needn't be a master wordsmith to score impressive sales with editors, who are often as inexperienced with crossword puzzles as you are now. To find real success in crosswording, you must be among the first to approach an editor, to place the first puzzle in his company or fraternal organization magazine or his tourist guide. In doing so, you'll earn several times the five-dollar to twenty-dollar fee routinely paid by newspapers and other traditional markets. To succeed, all you need are a few basic rules of construction, a good dictionary and supporting word books, and knowledge of the shortcuts available to all crossworders. Then it's a matter of slanting your work to find a high-paying home.

Here are the only clues you'll need to successfully solve the puzzle of crosswords: (1) Draw the diagram; (2) Number the boxes; (3) Select and insert the interlocking words; (4) Write the definitions; and (5) Find and sell to the markets.

Completing a fifteen-square-wide puzzle, including drawing the diagram, takes from five to fifteen hours. The diagram is the arrangement of black boxes in juxtaposition with white boxes—or *outs*—placed symmetrically on a grid. The blacked-in diagram is often called the *design* or *pattern*.

Always complete the pattern before writing in the words. The ratio of outs to white boxes should be one to six, meaning a standard fifteen-box square (fifteen boxes wide by fifteen boxes deep) won't include more than thirty-six or thirty-seven outs. Also, every box should be part of two words—one vertical and one horizontal. A well-constructed crossword has no unkeyed boxes—that is, letters that are part of only one word. In the most discriminating markets, editors further insist that the puzzle contain no two-letter words. But in the markets I'll show you how to tap, most editors don't object to a few of these short terms (although no more than four).

A crossworder once wrote in *Writer's Digest* that he seldom spent any time drawing a diagram. He merely tore the design from the magazine or newspaper, recopied it on manuscript paper, and inserted his own new words. I do the same. It is perfectly legal, since diagrams—like titles—can't be copyrighted. Clues and words transform the puzzle into a protectable whole.

Once the design is complete, place numbers in each box containing the first letter of horizontal and vertical words. About half will serve a dual purpose, marking the start of both a horizontal and a vertical word. If you have lifted your diagram from another source, you will use the same numbering system as the original. The numbers should be instantly legible. Use a typewriter to insert them.

As with diagrams, shortcuts are available as you fill in the letters. I have a notebook of completed word squares—the 3x3 (that is, three letters across by three letters down) to 6x6 blocks of letters that anchor the corners of most puzzles. Some of these I constructed, but most were copied from other crosswords. (My *Word Squares and Other Word Forms* collects about 2,000 squares. It's available for five dollars from National Library Publications, Box 73, Brooklyn, New York 11234.) These squares can help complete or begin those obstinate corners and same many precious minutes.

Twisting is a common practice with these squares, although many established editors consider it an undesirable one. By twisting, or changing, the position of words (vertical lines are read horizontally and vice versa) and substituting letters, I can change a square to something entirely different. New clues complete the transformation. It's the clues that make the puzzle different, aided by a theme. This technique is especially helpful in selling nearly identical puzzles to unrelated markets.

Let's look at a sample 4x4 square.

```
M O R E
E V I L
L E S S
T R E E
```

I twist this box by exchanging the vertical and horizontal lines. I can then substitute *C* for *M*, *A* for *O*, and *O* for *E* once each (*MORE* became *CARE* and *EVIL* became *OVIL*). The result:

```
C O L T
A V E R
R I S E
E L S E
```

CROSSING WORDS

Even if you use word squares to start or complete your puzzle, you'll need more help to fill in the remainder of the puzzle. The easiest process is the stepladder or diagonal method which enables the crossworder to unite his endings easily and to quickly put together the central part of a large diagram.

Several resources should be at hand to fill the blocks of your design with letters. The first is a dependable dictionary (unabridged volumes are nice, but any college edition will do). You will also need one or more specially grouped word books. One of the best is *Instant Word Finder* (distributed by National Library Publications). Culled from three dictionaries, the works are arranged in alphabetical order based on the needed letter. With this book, you won't ever discard a half-finished puzzle because you can't find an eight-letter word whose fifth letter is *o*. Looking in the correct column, you'll find more than 120 words presented alphabetically on each side of the letter in question—including *clam-o-rer, enam-o-red, prem-o-rse, trim-o-rph*, and *nonm-o-ral*.

Just as handy as any reference book is this nonsensical group of letters: *e, t, a, o, i, n, s, h, r, d, l, u*, the most-used letters in the alphabet. Look for and use words containing them. Letters like *x, z, q, v, g, k*, and a few others, appearing in the middle of a word, will usually create difficulties as you try to cross them with other words.

E, t, a, o, i, n, and *s* are good beginning letters, and with the exception of *o* and *a*, are also suited for the ends of words. Words like *animated* and *catamaran* are excellent choices because of the alternation of vowels and consonants. But a word like *beautiful* is not helpful, because its three consecutive vowels will complicate crossings. A word like *schmaltz* is a crossworder's curse, containing only one vowel and seven consonants—including four that are not among the six most commonly used letters.

As important as the words that fill your puzzle are the definitions that will provide the clues to your audience. Definitions should be as terse as possible, but also thought-provoking. Editors cringe at clues like "One who runs" for the word *runner*. That's equivalent to shouting the answer. It's better to define that word as "A climbing plant" or "A messenger." Also avoid verbs that end in *s* and plurals with their giveaway definitions—such as "Headgear (plural)" for *hats*.

When writing clues, start with the horizontal words. Begin each definition on a separate line with a capital letter. Keep your clues in tempo with the target publication and don't be afraid to inject humor. By all means, *do not* depend on your memory when defining words. If you have any doubt at all, look it up. It's also customary to list the source of your spellings and definitions, especially if you use unusual terms in the puzzle.

CONSTRUCTING A SALE

My greatest successes as a freelance crossworder have come from being the first to approach the editor of a new magazine or newspaper with a specially slanted puzzle. I once noticed in the advertising column of *The New York Times* (*Folio* magazine also has been a helpful source) the announcement of a new magazine to be distributed aboard six cruise ships. I immediately prepared a partial puzzle slanted toward cruise ships, added samples of my previous work, and queried the editor to see if he would consider an original crossword with a cruise theme. I offered to complete my thirteen-square rough draft for sixty dollars. The editor accepted and requested additional crosswords. I opened another market when I picked up a copy of a religious magazine in a New York City subway and noticed it lacked a crossword. I contacted the publisher and received an immediate acceptance, along with the opportunity to submit other fillers. (Many times a crossworder has an inside track on selling poetry and other fillers regularly.)

Such incidents often happen to me. And they can for you, as well. You need only seek, find, develop, and retain your own personal buyers. But where can a beginner find them?

How about the 4,000 publications produced by private firms? Mailed to customers and patrons, or handed to employees, many would include original crosswords if they were made available to the editors. These editors would also pay more than the traditional markets because the puzzle has been custom-created—slanted in several ways to their special interests, products, or services. These publications are listed in *Internal Publications Directory,* volume five of *The Working Press of the Nation* (available in most public libraries).

What about the thousands of hotels that distribute tourist guides to their patrons? Their editors always need appropriate material, and if properly themed, crosswords can fill that need. I have created and sold puzzles to several, including *Bay Area Guide,* which once engaged me for a whole year. Visit the more prestigious local hotels for samples of these guides. Then contact the editor.

Consider also the hundreds of fraternal, military, recreational, and religious associations in the United States, such as the Masons, Veterans of Foreign Wars, Oddfellows, Lions Clubs, and Rotary Clubs—each with numerous lodges, chapters, posts, and units across the country. Add to that thousands of other associations and organizations, all potential markets because they publish a newsletter, magazine, or newspaper for members. A crossword constructor can create a syndicate to feed these markets by providing specially geared crosswords to individual publications coast to coast. I've also found a steady market in the souvenir journals these groups issue to mark conventions and other meetings. I make the crossword special by sprinkling the names of officers and founders throughout the puzzle, and I have sold such puzzles for $75 to $200 each. In most cases, I get repeat orders. Five organizations are still buying puzzles from me after ten years. The *Encyclopedia of Associations* (available in most public libraries) annually publishes an extensive listing of such groups.

There's an international market for crosswords in the newspapers and magazines published by the more than 1,000 American corporations that maintain offices overseas. Before Libya nationalized its oil fields, the Arabian-American Oil Company published a weekly newspaper that included my original crosswords. Nearly every corporation listed in *Fortune*'s 500 operates overseas, and the International Trade Commission (701 E Street NW, Washington, D.C. 20436) may provide a more extensive listing.

Closer to home, look to the local shopping mall's or business district's guide to merchants. An acquaintance of mine established a limited personal syndicate by selling the same puzzle each week to more than a dozen shopping papers across the country. *The 1987 IMS Directory of Publications* (available in most public libraries) can guide you to the many advertising-oriented shoppers, while the *Shopping Center Directory* (available in most public libraries) can put you in contact with retail center marketing directors.

When mailing queries to prospective buyers, enclose samples of your puzzles. But also fill in part of a fresh diagram with words and clues slanted to that market.

Like you, the editors of these publications are looking for the right combination to fill white spaces. While you are placing letters in small white boxes, they are seeking features to entertain their readers. Provide them with an original crossword puzzle to fill their space and they'll reward you with a series of letters that spell success—your name on an acceptance check.

How to Write and Sell Greeting Cards

Patricia Ann Emme

If you think receiving a nice greeting card is heartwarming, wait until you start receiving checks for *writing* those cards.

Can you imagine receiving $500 just for writing ten inspirational poems, or $25 for writing only one line of prose? I can, because I have made many such sales.

I began writing for the greeting card industry in 1956. Since then, I've sold thousands of card ideas to the various companies who buy freelance material. I've also sold verses to many of the card companies that don't usually buy material from freelance writers.

Every verse that can easily be adapted and used for many different occasions is a Godsend to editors. The following inspirational of mine was purchased thirty years ago. It has since appeared on wedding and anniversary cards, Valentine's Day cards, and holiday cards for husbands, wives, and sweethearts to send to each other.

God's Greatest Gift . . . The Gift of Love!

> When love is true
> The bluebirds sing,
> And even winter seems like spring . . .
> When love is true
> The days hold cheer,
> And all life's worries disappear   . .
> When love is true
> The heart is strong
> And all the world sings Love's sweet song . . .
> A precious gift

From up above . . .
God's greatest gift, The Gift of Love.

Even though editors buy a lot of four- and eight-line verses for their every-day line, the inspirational verse is still in great demand. Editors never get enough well-written inspirationals. Hallmark, American Greetings, Para-mount, Warner Press, and Freedom are only a few of the major companies that use inspirational verse.

Even though most well-established companies have large staffs of writers and artists who compose most of the cards for them, a good freelance writer *can* sell to these markets; and besides, hundreds of new card companies enter the market every year.

Studio cards are another area to explore. A studio card—also called a *contemporary* card—is upbeat, with a humorous or sentimental approach. The message is usually presented as two-line prose; the first line appears on the cover of the card, and the punch line appears inside. For example: "You're the cat's meow" on the outside; inside, "Purrfect . . . in every way!" Or, the sweet, sentimental approach: Outside, "I wish we were together now"; inside, "I really need something beautiful to brighten up my life."

From time to time, you'll also see specialized offbeat cards on the racks. Note the publishers' names and watch *Writer's Market* for information about their needs. Some do not accept freelance submissions but have their own artists/writers under contract for special lines.

Another type of humorous-card idea is writing something for the person who is only sending a card, and not purchasing a gift for someone, as in the following:

(outside)   I had to break open my favorite piggy bank just to buy you
             this card
(inside)   So you'd better be crazy about it!

Most studio ideas will bring you ten dollars, but many of the larger companies may pay twenty-five dollars or fifty dollars for a good two-line idea.

Because it usually accompanies an appropriate photograph or painting, another popular type of prose writing is known in the industry as *soft touch* or *image* idea.

Here is an example of this type of writing:

(outside)   When you walked out of my life
(inside)   So did all the love and caring!

The best way to get ideas for *any* type of card is to study the published cards in the stores. Also, you can learn to make lists of expressions that you hear or say that are complimentary, humorous, etc. Some of the things you might write down and write something around are as follows:

1. *I'm so glad we could spend today together.*
2. *I like you more than I like anyone else.*
3. *You have the gift of being able to make everyone feel important.*
4. *I don't know what I'd do without you.*

The list is endless because it is the everyday things that we say and feel that make the best greeting card material.

Card companies also purchase plaque ideas, motto buttons, bumper sticker sayings, and inspirational material that can be used for special occasions. Office workers and people with a good sense of humor often purchase this type of material.

Some examples of this type of writing are:

(for an office worker)	My boss is intelligent, handsome, and a great judge of character. HE HIRED ME, DIDN'T HE!
(for the diet-conscious)	Dieting rotted my brain. Now I'm skinny and stupid!
(desk plaque)	Anyone who can wear a smile all the time is either loony or in a coma!
(bumper sticker)	Don't you dare laugh at my car, it's grouchy enough already!

For humorous buttons that people like to wear, you might try something like the following:

If anyone can make a man out of me . . . YOU CAN!
If you date me you'll really know what fear is!

For inspirational-type plaques, the following is an example of what editors look for.

True Love

True love is the candle
That burns in the night
Outshining the stars' glow
Because it's so bright.

There are plaques for friendship, faith, strength, mother and father, special sister or brother, and a variety of others. Study what the stores are selling and you'll come up with many ideas of your own.

Now to get to the most popular verses that appear on more than half the published cards. These are known as staples in the industry because they are used over and over again by editors—some in boxed assortments, others on counter cards; many remain in a card line for thirty years or more.

The majority of these are either four- or eight-line verses, perfectly rhymed and easy to sell.

Here is an example of the type that I have sold to editors on a regular basis:

(for practically all occasions)

> Today is such a perfect time
> To send a word to say
> I'm grateful for the love we share
> Today and every day.

As you can see, these verses all have perfect rhyme and meter. They are uplifting and easy to understand but not overly sentimental or mushy.

Companies like Warner Press, Paramount, Hallmark, and Gibson all have religious verses on some of their cards. Including a special Bible verse with your religious submissions can greatly enhance the verse. Thousands of people wouldn't think of sending a card unless it was religious in content, so think about this market if you are inclined to write inspirational material.

Whatever the type of card you write, read the already-published cards carefully to get an idea of what editors are buying. Pattern your early work after the published cards. Don't copy them, but do try to emulate their formats while developing your own style.

A good rhyming dictionary and a thesaurus are essential investments for a greeting card writer, because they help you write more effectively and precisely.

Get a notebook and begin writing down expressions and thoughts that you think you can work with. Example: Think about someone you would like to be with right now. What do you like about that person? How does that person make you feel when you're with him or her? What special thing would you like to give that person if you could?

Jot down ideas pertaining to a specific season, holiday, or event.

Consult books of quotations, classic poetry, and other such volumes for ideas. And learn to pay attention to the rest of the world—even song titles can spark your imagination. The popular song "You Light up My Life" inspired me to write, "You don't only light up my life . . . you light up the whole world," which earned me twenty-five dollars.

Submit your verse or ideas on index cards—one idea to a card. Type your name and address in the upper left-hand corner, and number your verse in the upper right. This will help both you and the card company keep track of submissions. Then type your verse, centering the title. Double-space verses that are four lines or shorter. For longer poems, use larger index cards.

Use a file-card system to keep track of your submissions. Prepare a 3x5 card for each idea, and list all submission details on that card.

Submit greeting card verses in batches of about fifteen. Ask the company if it has a *tip sheet* that describes the company's current needs. Tip sheets are published regularly, so see if you can get on the company's mailing list.

Most card companies buy all rights to material from a freelance writer. In the event that you wish to include some of your published greeting-card-verse material in an article or book-length manuscript, most greeting card editors will give you permission provided that you credit the company that purchased the particular verse, etc., that you are including in your book or article. Once all rights to a verse or idea have been sold, it is no longer your property. It belongs to the company that purchased it.

You might want to order a subscription to *Greetings Magazine*, which comes out every month. It is the official buyer's guide for the greeting card industry, and it contains valuable information for greeting card writers and artists. You can write to them at the following address: Greetings Magazine, 309 Fifth Avenue, New York, New York 10016.

And remember: Don't be discouraged if your first attempts at writing fail. I started out writing only inspirationals, and today I write not only for the card companies, but also for magazines, church bulletins, hymn writers, and others. I have learned to write short stories, fillers for magazines, how-to articles, and more. Some of my poetry has been used on radio broadcasts and included in church sermons all over the country.

It's nice to receive a greeting card in the mail, but a greeting card with your words on it—and a check with your name on it—is the nicest greeting of all.

Cartoon Gagwriting Is No Laughing Matter . . . or Is It?

Carl Wells and Barry Gantt

Cartoon gagwriting is a way for someone with an eye for humor to generate additional income. For example, some idle speculation one afternoon about sharks in swimming pools eventually led author Wells to a sale to *The Saturday Evening Post* and his share of the cartoonist's fee: a wallet-fattening $31.25. The caption was twelve words, so that's more than $2.50 per word—not bad.

Cartoon humor springs from daydreams, random musings, and reflections on the incongruities, ironies, and oddities of life. These things have inspired us to write gags that we have placed with a number of cartoonists who, in turn, have sold the final product to magazines ranging from *Playboy* to *Saturday Review*. If your brain regularly serves up the offbeat and ridiculous, there just might be cartoon sales (and dollars) in *your* future, too.

It doesn't matter that you can't draw even a simple stick figure, because professional cartoonists are looking for fresh, clever, *funny* ideas that lend themselves to a magazine cartoon format. Personal contact isn't necessary—we have found that partnership with these cartoonists is as close as the nearest mailbox.

Boston-area writer Harald Bakken estimates that more than 80 percent of all cartoonists use writers at least some of the time. Bakken, whose sales include *The New Yorker, Saturday Review, Parade,* and many other major magazines, explains: "Cartoonists may feel they're good at drawing, but not so good at creating ideas. Particularly if they're full-time cartoonists, they may not have time to generate the volume of ideas they need to draw and sell in order to survive. They may want to sell to specialized magazines in fields about which they know little. Or they may hit a dry spell in their own creativity with gags and use writers for a time to tide them over." A list of cartoonists seeking gags appears in each edition of *Writer's Market*.

Cartoon writers, then, meet a definite need by supplying a flow of original ideas to cartoonists. Here's how it works, in brief: First, you type up your funny ideas on gagslips (3x5 cards) and send them to the cartoonist. He selects the ones he believes to have good sales potential, holds these, and sends back the rest. Next, he draws up the "holds" and markets them to magazines (and certain newspapers), sometimes redrawing them to editors' specifications. If a cartoon wins final approval, the editor pays the cartoonist, who in turn forwards a portion of the payment for each cartoon to you. Smiles all around.

The standard writer payment is 25 percent of what the cartoonist receives. This percentage reflects the significant time and effort spent by the cartoonist in drawing (and redrawing) the cartoon as well as the costs of art supplies and marketing (cartoonists, as do writers, keep a fearful eye on postal rates). In the case of the occasional reprint in a textbook or other publication, the writer is compensated again.

As you build your contacts and a record of sales emerges, your writer's rate of payment may rise to 30 percent and higher. Cartoonists are usually quite willing to negotiate increases with writers who consistently supply top gags.

Your share of the loot can range from a couple of bucks for a sale to a small regional trade journal to $200 + for hitting the highest-paying national magazines.

Magazines pay widely varying rates to cartoonists for use of their work. Major magazines with large national circulations pay the best, of course. A cartoon placed with *Good Housekeeping*, for example, might earn $200; *Reader's Digest*, $125; *Playboy*, $350; *The New Yorker*, $200 + ; and *Boys' Life*, $75. Keep in mind that these fees listed are typical of the magazines—individual artists often earn much higher rates (sometimes through special contractual arrangements); fees may be open to negotiation and may vary according to size of drawing and placement in the magazine; and rates at a particular magazine may fluctuate.

The smaller magazines with more limited circulations and resources pay much lower rates: $10, $15, and $25 payments are quite common. Then there are the magazines that are labors of love, of course, and are able to pay only in contributors' copies.

Cartoon writers find, then, that their incomes are most often characterized by a certain number of sales to major, general-circulation magazines and a larger number of sales to smaller magazines, often trade journals or specialty publications.

Just a few sales to "the majors" will put several hundred dollars into your checking account. Of course, competition is stiff for cartoon sales to these publications, and you will have to write your funniest. Smaller checks will generate income more slowly but more steadily. Some hard-working writers earn several thousands of dollars per year of part-time income through gagwriting, but only a rare few support themselves through cartoon writing alone, and these are especially talented and dedicated people. For a beginning cartoon writer, the sensible approach is to keep your regular source of income as you try your hand at the biz.

Gagwriter Ronnie Johnson, for instance, with a record of sales including *Playboy, Cosmopolitan, The Saturday Evening Post,* and the *Wall Street Journal,* supplements his regular post office job with an average of $100 per week cartoon writing income. He produces funny material for syndicated newspaper features, one of which is the popular Frank and Ernest panel by Bob Thaves. Johnson's close business relationship with cartoonists demonstrates the benefit of making yourself known as a professional, reliable source of good material.

We rely on other sources of income, too, but gagwriting provides a healthy increase to our yearly earnings. Gantt earns 25 percent of his income from gagwriting. Wells's percentage isn't as high, but his experience in polishing gaglines has helped him market prose humor to newspapers around the country.

WHAT'S SELLING NOW?

As in other forms of writing, you increase the likelihood of making sales by studying successful products in the marketplace to see what makes them effective.

"What sets the cartoon apart from other art forms is exaggeration," cartoonist Roy Paul Nelson says. "A cartoon screams, while an ordinary drawing or painting whispers. The exaggeration involves the idea as well as the drawing."

You will find, as we have, that there is no one formula for sure-fire humor—many a cartoon may seem truly to be one-of-a-kind. But as you observe the wide variety of styles and subjects, certain plots or categories become apparent.

One such plot is the familiar phrase, dear to the hearts of cartoon writers everywhere. For example, by introducing an unexpected variation on a familiar phrase, author Gantt wrote this chicken-coop scene—Hen with rooster announces to hen on nest: "We've decided not to have eggs." Result? A check for twenty-five dollars and a nice sale to *Saturday Review*.

Here are some other idea categories with recent examples of ideas that turned us a profit:

Satire

Cop gives citation to driver of LeCar: "And especially for you, 'le ticket.' " (Gantt in *Mother Jones*)

Fantasy

Frog with straw hat and striped coat sits on stool and sings with other members of barbershop quartet. Observer to same: "All I know is they were sure glad to find someone who could sing bass and come to practice every Tuesday night." (Wells in *Christian Science Monitor*)

Understatement

Swimming coach threatens to cut leash holding shark in pool. Swimmer swims frantically away. Observer to same: "A bit unorthodox in his training methods perhaps . . . but he wins meets." (Wells in *The Saturday Evening Post*)

Exaggeration

Four windows at Post Office. One reads "Stamps"; *three* read "Complaints." (Gantt in *The Wall Street Journal*)

Literal

Robin to hummingbird: "You mean to say you never knew any of the words?" (Wells in *Wisconsin Agriculturist*)

Reverse

Woman sits in rocking chair. "Son" is tattooed on her forearm. (Wells in *The Wall Street Journal*)

Ridiculous

Two swallows hitchhiking. One has suitcase labeled, "Capistrano." (Gantt in the *San Francisco Bay Guardian*)

DEVELOPING THE IDEA

Idea creation is sparked in hundreds of different ways, so always keep a notebook handy. Nothing is more infuriating than losing a big one because of your own failure to write it down. As welcome as those unbidden flashes of inspiration are, though, you will need something more dependable if you want to produce ideas regularly.

    Cartoon writers have many favorite ways of generating ideas. Some writers are newspaper perusers, finding a wealth of ideas lurking in every section of the daily newspaper; some get ideas at the movies; others swear by television, especially Johnny Carson's *The Tonight Show.*

Keep a log of puns and funny headlines extracted from newspapers and magazines. Some magazines even have sections where almost every headline is some form of wordplay. *Time* is laced with these items, and many can be spun off into setups for gags.

Two idea-stimulation techniques have proved especially effective for us. One is the "Ingredients for Gag Recipes" chart discussed by Jack Markow in his *Cartoonist's and Gag Writer's Handbook.* The first column of this chart lists people—plumber, astronomer, chicken plucker, gorilla (animals are people too), king, and so on. The second column includes places, such as North Pole, lighthouse, covered wagon, outdoor cafe. The third column lists props, such as income tax form, sunglasses, bongo drums, stilts. By matching two or more ingredients from the chart, you can give shape to an idea. Many writers use charts they design themselves, filling them with ingredients applicable to the type of gags their cartoonists usually use. A writer specializing in medical gags, for instance, would populate his chart with such ingredients as doctors, pharmacists, operating tables, and so on.

The other successful technique we use is *switching,* which involves looking at published cartoons and changing the situation or the gagline so that a new, original gag is produced. Note the term *original.* Your new gag uses the same or a similar premise, but must involve a substitution.

Switching is an accepted practice; so accepted, in fact, that gagwriter John Dromey recently pointed to some published gags to show how it works:

Original cartoon: Doctor to patient: "Well, let's put it this way—if you were a horse, you'd have to be shot."

Switched cartoon: Doctor to farmer: "In other words, if you were a tractor tire, I wouldn't recap."

Further switch: Auto mechanic to owner of car in shop for repairs: "Let's put it this way—how do you feel about public transportation?"

Collections of cartoons in the library are a great source of inspiration for us. They are usually found in the art department or in general reference. Lariar's *Best of the Year* collections are good, as are *The New Yorker* collections and various collections of individual artists' work. When going through these, either switch ideas from one format or scene to another, or else try covering up the caption and substituting your own (and funnier!) idea.

Slanting your thinking toward a particular group of markets can help ideas flow more easily. Let's say that you're writing for a cartoonist who draws cartoons for the *medicals,* magazines for people in the medical profession. Some are aimed at doctors, some at nurses, some at hospital administrators, others at lab technicians, and still others, at specializations within these target groups. You won't find cartoons portraying a cynical view toward doctor's fees in *Friendly Ole Physician Magazine* or cartoons using the specialized terminology of the pharmaceutical industry in a magazine for hospital-equipment sales-people.

Leaf through the magazines at the library, and you will find fodder for ideas as well as get a feel for the tone and scope of the magazines. Read over an editorial or two; glance at the article titles and subjects. You will begin to get ideas, and you will increase your confidence that the gags you write are right for the market. Find out which magazines cartoonists sell to regularly, and aim your material at those markets. Gantt slanted one of his gags to *Writer's Digest,* and cartoonist Grant Canfield sold the cartoon: Angel sits writing at desk perched on cloud. Sign on desk says *Religious Editor.* Three-tiered in-basket labeled *up, limbo,* and *down* sits on desk.

As you make yourself known as a reliable source of funny material for specific markets, cartoonists may begin to give you special writing assignments, for example, "Dear Writer: The editor at a travel magazine I regularly sell to wants me to do a special, cartoon feature page for next July's issue, so I'll need gags about packing, lost luggage, airports, train stations, hotels, taxis, sight-seeing, souvenirs—anything about the pleasures and perils of traveling. The magazine's readers are family-oriented, and the slant is on domestic rather than overseas travel. See what you can come up with for me." Assignments like this help focus your creative energies on specific types of gags.

Cartoon Captions and Descriptions

One of the rewarding features of cartoon writing is that writer's cramp is practically unheard of. Writer's twinge, maybe. An idea may be slow to come, but when it does, you are only about fifteen words from having it all down on paper.

There are two parts to getting it down: one is the caption itself (if the gag is not solely visual), and the other is the description of the cartoon that you will use to convey your idea to the cartoonist.

First the caption: Generally, the shorter the better. Long captions of more than, say, twenty words tend to distract the reader. Most cartoons are designed for readers' quick uptake; their primary impact is visual. Even cartoons that are basically illustrated jokes lose some of their punch if the reader must wade through a quarter-page of prose to find out what is funny.

Gagwriters, like their cousins the poets, work to make every word count. A classic cartoon scene is the one showing some panorama of destruction after a person's sneeze. Let's picture, for example, a pillow factory employee—a pillow-stuffer—standing in a cloud of goose feathers. The foreman deadpans, "Gesundheit." Longer captions such as "I hope that you get over your cold soon" or "That was some sneeze, Carlyle" lose effectiveness.

To help make the caption sparkle, use words that have a bit of built-in humor value. *Tiddlywink, girdle,* and *pickle,* for instance, never hurt your laugh potential. They won't substitute for the basic funny idea, but they *will* embroider it. Look for those interesting-sounding words with "a little devil" in them. One such word, used repeatedly, made the point in a recent *New Yorker* cartoon: Books on a shelf are titled: *Mumbo-Jumbo Legal, Mumbo-Jumbo Medical, Mumbo-Jumbo Political,* etc. (cartoonist Dana Fradon).

If you're a lousy speller and punctuation makes you shudder, you will need some reference sources handy. Remember that the punctuation of the written words in a cartoon caption plays the same role as timing in the spoken words of a stand-up comic's routine.

The second part to getting down your idea is the description for the cartoonist. Here, too, you don't need extra words. One-panel ideas (cartoons with only one scene, as opposed to multipanel cartoons such as those found in comic strips) can almost always be explained satisfactorily in two or three lines. Instead of "There are two bearded men wearing shredded clothing. They are stranded on a desert island, lying under the island's only palm tree. Some coconuts are on the sand. One man says . . ." write this: "Desert island. Shipwrecked man to second . . ." Instead of writing: "An unshaven man who hasn't had water for days is crawling along the desert, when he discovers a water hole. In the water is . . ." write: "Desert crawler comes across water hole with tiny oil tanker, wrecked and spilling oil, floating in it." Simple and effective. But don't write that exact gag. Gantt has already used it, and cartoonist Tom Stratton turned the gag into a sale to *High Times.*

To launch your first effort, send a small batch of perhaps five gags (five great ones, and don't forget SASE!) to the cartoonist. Begin with one cartoonist, who may like to receive a new batch weekly, biweekly, or monthly. If you can produce more gags, contact more artists. Remember that the measure is how many sales you are making, not how many cartoonists you are supplying. Keep the quality of your gags at a professional level.

Chances are you won't have to wait long for a response. Most cartoonists are amazingly speedy, and a reply within the week isn't uncommon.

GAG ORDERS

Good advice from good gagwriters:

Rex May (sales to *Good Housekeeping, Reader's Digest,* and *The Christian Science Monitor*): "Buy all your materials—paper, pens, envelopes—in bulk quantities. Not only do you save money that way, but the very fact of 5,000 envelopes sitting in the corner makes you feel guilty if you don't get to work and use them up.

"Force yourself into a schedule, and don't make excuses for yourself. I write 300 gags per week. I'm told that some others write as many or more, but most gagwriters write fewer. The important thing is the goal—50 a week, or whatever.''

Harald Bakken (sales to *The New Yorker, Medical Economics,* and *New Woman*): ''For years, I've had an alliterative motto for this business: Be prolific, be persistent, and be patient. Prolific: Only a small percentage of your ideas will eventually sell. Volume is the only way to make money in this game. Persistent: If you believe in an idea, keep it in the mail. Eventually, someone will think it's funny. A recent case in point: Nineteen cartoonists rejected one of my ideas. The twentieth took it and within a month had sold it for $200 to *Cosmopolitan.* Patient: Marketing takes time. One well-known and well-paying magazine in the field has been known to take up to eight months to consider material. If your cartoonist is a consistent marketer, wait it out together.''

Terry Ryan (sales to *Saturday Review, Boy's Life,* and *Nutrition Health Review*): ''Brevity is all-important. Gagwriters, because they are writers, often make the mistake of being verbose in captions. Pare the gag down to its bare essentials. If possible, take brevity a step further into silence—wordless, visual gags are quite popular, and because of their simplicity, are usually difficult to conceive.

''Finally, construct the caption carefully so that the punch part of the gag falls at the end, and therefore, achieves the maximum effect.''

Next time you're yukking it up over a cartoon in your favorite magazine, remember that the cartoon probably put a smile on a writer's face, too. A check will do that, you know.

MAGAZINES FOR GAGWRITERS

These trade journals help working cartoon writers stay abreast of the latest market news and information.

The Gag Re-Cap, Box 86, East Meadow, New York 11554. Editor: Al Gottlieb. Monthly; $40/year, latest issue $5, back issue, $3. This publication gives verbal descriptions of cartoons appearing in most of the major and middle-market magazines during the previous month. It's useful for keeping track of who sells where, checking if your material has been sold, and stimulating ideas. It also provides an occasional forum for writers in the business. Editor also publishes an annual, *Directory of Cartoonists,* $8.

CARTOONIST PROfiles, Box 325, Farifield, Connecticut 06430. Editor: Jud Hurd. Quarterly; $12/year. It focuses mainly on working methods of cartoonists and comic-strip artists, but it's also useful as background information to sell with these artists.

The Idea Exchange, PO Box 99, Brandon, Vermont 05733. Editor: Lew Little.

Quarterly; $25/year, back issue, $7. This new quarterly is aimed at writers and cartoonists hoping to break into national syndication. It is published by Little, one of the most respected comic-strip editor/packagers in the country (was the driving force behind the success of *Garfield*).

CAMOC Newsletter, Cartoon Art Museum, Suite 205, 1 Sutter Street, San Francisco, California 94104. Editor: Ron Schwartz. Quarterly; free with annual membership to museum, $25/year. The emphasis is on background information on West Coast cartoonists and current exhibits; it also publishes news of regular arts-marketing conferences.

Cartoon World, Box 30367, Lincoln, Nebraska 68510. Editor: George Hartman. Monthly; $40/year, sample copy $5. Listings of the small-trade-journal and newsletter markets, as well as some biographical features, are published here.

Ten Christmas Gifts Only Writers Can Give

John McCollister

Uncle Willie gives me fits. I have never seen him wear any of the ties I have given him for Christmas over the years. But what do I usually end up buying him? A tie. I can't think of anything else.

I'm not alone in my frustrations. Just about everyone shares this problem—what to give friends and relatives without that annual pilgrimage to the shopping mall to spend a small fortune on gifts that may go unused.

A while ago, however, I realized that as writers, we have a solution right at our fingertips. Instead of shelling out your hard-earned cash for another tie that your Uncle Willie really doesn't want, do what I am going to do this year: give him and the rest of your family and friends gifts that they will talk about for months—gifts that are extensions of yourself through writing. Consider, therefore, the following ideas that utilize your writing to express your love during this special season.

1.   Research and compile a family history. This can be anything from a major project—a "mini-*Roots*," so to speak—to a simple family tree listing family members with dates and places of birth.

Send copies to your relatives. Imagine the number of kinfolk who would appreciate this priceless treasure that is bound to be passed on for generations.

2.   Write a poem for someone you care about. There's something about poetry that best captures our deepest feelings. Perhaps nothing touches the heart more. Fancy it up a bit with an old picture frame or a freehand sketch. *Caution*: don't dedicate the same poem to more than one person. This trick has a nasty habit of catching up with you.

3. Highlight family photos. For your son or daughter, organize those photographs you have collected over the years that are now stuffed away in some musty box. Arrange them in chronological order beginning with the hospital "mug shots" through the snapshots taken over the past year. Relive those precious moments of your youngster at play . . . going to school . . . leaving on the first date . . . at graduation . . . Accompany each picture with a paragraph or two sharing your thoughts at the moment the camera clicked. In these commentaries, show how both of your attitudes have changed.

One mother I know used an interesting twist on this idea. The first year her daughter-in-law was in the family, she compiled a collection of pictures of her son in a photograph album, which she titled *This Is Your Husband's Life*.

4. Write letters for someone. Think of those you know who are physically unable to write—the sick, the aged, the blind. Some of these folks—especially the senior citizens—have fascinating stories to tell that might supplement your writing projects.

5. Create a family calendar. Using a standard calendar—one with blank squares for each date—record events such as birthdays, wedding anniversaries, upcoming graduations, and other important happenings on the horizon. What a terrific gift idea for those who are apt to let one or more of these days slip by.

Include a quote-of-the-month at the top of each page. You could get by with some quotes by famous people, but you might want to write your own thoughts or recall favorite expressions characteristic of family members. For as long as I can remember, my Uncle Ben, an avid fisherman, has looked out the window each morning at breakfast and asked, "Wonder how they're bitin' t'day." That daily question has been a "trademark" of Uncle Ben. I would use this as my quote-of-the-month for April when the trout season begins.

6. Describe sentimental items. Do you still have a pair of Grandpa's glasses tucked away in a dresser drawer? Who in the family admired him enough to cherish this remembrance? Is your old church being remodeled? Would someone appreciate a piece of the furniture? What about that bookrack you used in college? Wouldn't your college-bound son or daughter value it?

Each of these items is meaningful, especially if you personalize the gift by accompanying it with your written description of the article. Describe its significance and why you chose to pass it along to this particular person.

7. Write a personalized children's story. Use your children, grandchildren, nieces, or nephews as the central figures, and include their close friends and playmates in supporting roles. Names of familiar streets and landmarks add another personal touch. Weave into the story meaningful dates such as a birthday or the first day of school.

By the way, you can use the same story line for more than one youngster by merely changing names and dates.

8. Send Christmas letters. Instead of mailing traditional Christmas cards, send creative, personal Yuletide greetings.

Your letters may tell of family happenings over the past year, or if you want to add some depth, contain reflections on such things as what Christmas means to you. You might even compose an original Christmas story.

9. Record your childhood memories. Include those special family traditions built up through the years. Use your skills in describing the *clippity-clop* of horse-drawn wagons on cobblestone streets, or the spicy aroma of pumpkin pies fresh from the oven. Trigger the imagination through vivid word pictures helping your audience to share those beautiful memories of long ago. Give this personal history to those who will treasure it—your parents, children, or grand-children.

10. Write a Christmas play for your local Sunday school. Here's a gift for the entire community.

What can you write that hasn't been said thousands of times before? Use your imagination. For example, what would have happened were the Christ child born in the twentieth century in your town? How would the news media report it? What would be the reaction of your neighbors?

Include speaking parts for as many youngsters as possible. Suggest stage directions and scene and costume designs, as well as any music that would accent your narrative.

Remember, this is for children, so keep your thoughts big but your words small.

There you have it—ten gifts you can give this Christmas that cost only a few hours. Yet, each gift is personal, comes from the heart, and will be appreciated.

So, this year it's a family calendar for Uncle Willie. Not only will I be giving him a gift he can use, but I can also use the money I save to buy myself a new tie.

GIFT RAP

Things to keep in mind while preparing your gifts:

1. Give yourself plenty of time. You can't begin too early preparing your gifts through writing skills. Rushing to meet a deadline only a few days away

does little for quality. These gifts cost little in terms of money; your investment of time, however, should not be skimped on.

2. Save the material you write. Don't toss it away with the Christmas gift wrappings. Even though your messages may be personal, some may come in handy for your other writing. For example, your childhood memories may provide a realistic background for a short story or novel.

3. Use photographs. If you have a good camera and a talent for using one, take pictures that highlight your gift. A family history comes alive even more with pictures of the characters.

Pictures also supplement your magazine-article submissions. Editors are quick to admit that an article accompanied by a sharp, black-and-white glossy photo stands a better chance of being accepted.

4. A tape recorder helps. If your gift involves extensive research, a compact cassette recorder is ideal for interviews. It sure beats frantically trying to catch every word.

Be sure to save these recordings. Voices become more precious as the years pass, especially when some of the folks you have interviewed are no longer around. The recordings may eventually become gifts themselves.

My First Sale: It Pays to Be a Reader

Pat Sobleskie

My first sale required neither research nor query letter, was published in a national publication, and paid fifty dollars for an hour's work. Sounds too good to be true? Perhaps. But it happened.

Anyone who has ever read a magazine has probably come across reader-contribution sections, sometimes called *personal essays*. These are the page or pages in a magazine in which the editor invites readers to contribute certain features, such as: "*Grit* welcomes 400-word opinion pieces for this column (As I See It) on topics of national interest." (They pay thirty-five dollars.) In fact, editors who publish these reader features are very receptive to them, according to *Reader's Digest*'s senior staff editor, Regina Grant Hersey; in her words, "Our readers' experiences give a fresh, honest, and very human look at what is amusing in life. The departments that carry reader anecdotes are some of the most popular in the magazine." Yet *Reader's Digest,* the largest user of reader contributor material, is not the only magazine that uses these features—quite the contrary.

Many national publications welcome readers to contribute a wide range of article types and experiences. These features include jokes, prayers, opinions, cooking and household tips, recipes, quotes, light verse, and an assortment of inspirational, humorous, and informative articles and anecdotes. For example: "Tell us about your favorite Ford. We pay $100. . . ." (*Ford Times*).

Reader contribution sections can be found in just about every market—religious (*Guideposts, Catholic Digest*); general interest (*Reader's Digest, Grit, Ford Times, National Enquirer, Newsweek, Southern Living*); confession (*True Confessions, True Romance, Modern Romance, True Story*); writer's publications (*Writer's Digest, Byline*); and probably the most lucrative market, women's publications (*Redbook, Complete Woman, Family Circle, Woman's Day, Ladies' Home Journal, Cosmopolitan, Savvy,* and others).

But how does a beginning writer find the magazines that use reader-contribution sections? The writer, quite naturally, must be (as the title suggests) a *reader,* as I discovered with my first sale.

I was reading Norman Vincent Peale's *Guideposts* magazine (with no intention of writing for the inspirational publication) when I spotted a small inset on the bottom of one of the pages. According to the italicized print, the editor was inviting readers to submit devotional thoughts for the upcoming edition of *Daily Guideposts,* an annual hardcover. The format was simple—a short quotation followed by a related anecdote, ending with a one-line prayer. Contributors whose work was accepted would be paid fifty dollars.

I was reluctant to contribute. Although I had seen numerous reader-contribution features in various magazines, I didn't think they applied to me. After all, I was a *serious* writer, not your average reader. I often pictured editors of such features pulling their hair out trying to decipher these bits of reader trivia written on scraps of notebook paper, flowery stationery, or typed (single-spaced) on erasable bond. Besides, I always dreamed that my first sale would be a 4,000-word, heavily researched article published in a major national magazine and rewarding me with a generous check. But even dreamers have their moments of reality and resignation. Swallowing my pride and emerging from the depths of professional snobbery, I decided, why not?

Choosing friendship as my theme, I used an anecdote about Abraham Lincoln befriending a lonely Confederate prisoner-of-war. I picked a familiar quote from Emerson: "The only way to have a friend is to be one." Then I made up a prayer (for the submission as well as for myself). I typed it, enclosed an SASE, mailed it, and waited. Several weeks later, I received a congratulatory note informing me that my submission had been accepted. A check for fifty dollars soon followed.

From my first sale, I learned that it pays to be a reader, and I can give you seven reasons that you'll discover it, too.

1. *Reader-contribution features require little or no research.* Most of these features are true, first-person, slice-of-life pieces. Living makes up most of the research. Whether you've experienced a dramatic happening ("What was your most dramatic life-changing experience? Write it in 300 words or less . . . you will be paid twenty-five dollars"—*Grit),* a spiritual awakening ("For statements of true incidents through which people are brought into the Church or return to the faith, fifty dollars will be paid. . . ." —*Catholic Digest),* or whether you just enjoy writing about your everyday life ("Please tell us about your pet . . . we will pay you fifty dollars"—*True Story),* some editor is waiting to hear from you.

2. *Reader-contribution features require no query letter.* Just type the submission and mail it. Most reader-contribution sections state that submissions cannot be acknowledged or returned, if rejected. Many will return the submission if you include an SASE; however, some will not. (*Reader's Digest,* which receives about 1,000 contributions a day, will not return any reader-contributed material. If you haven't received an acceptance in ninety days, try your idea elsewhere.)

3. *Reader-contribution features are an excellent way to break into print on the national level.* After sending various query letters to *Ford Times* and to *Grit* in an attempt to break in, I succeeded (the first time) in breaking in at both publications through their reader-contribution sections (*Ford Times*'s "Road Show" section and *Grit*'s "Turning Point" column).

4. *Reader-contribution features give the beginning writer the same chance for publication as the seasoned professional.* According to *Grit*'s editor-in-chief, Naomi Woolever: "A professional writer would not have an advantage in the first-person participation articles. These articles represent a kind of journalism that is alternately folksy and inspirational. . . . One of the advantages [of such articles] is to show that people still have a language of their own in their own region."

5. *Some reader-contribution features pay very well. Redbook*'s "Young Mother's Story" pays $750 for 1,500- to 2,000-word, dramatic personal-experience pieces. *Woman's World* pays $250 for contributions to its "Turning Point" column. *Reader's Digest* pays $300 for amusing anecdotes. Most magazines pay an average of $25 to $50 for various features.

6. *Reader-contribution features are easy to write.* What could be easier than writing about the happenings of your life? The editor's instructions (word count, payment, and description of item, along with a published example) are always included on the magazine page. The time each takes is also minimal. (My first sale took an hour, at most.)

7. *Reader-contribution features contribute to a beginning writer's inspiration, productivity, and practice.* Even now, five years after my first sale, I still keep a watchful eye on reader-contribution sections to practice my craft, to generate ideas, and to feel productive. It's exciting to find a new market to send your work to, and nothing soothes the rejection blues better than sending out two or three reader features at a time. But more importantly, at the beginning, sending out work regularly made me feel like a writer. And, as most writers will agree, feeling like a writer is half the struggle of becoming one.

Now discover, as I did, that it pays to be a reader.

How to Enjoy Books, Theater, and the Movies— for Free!

Leonard L. Knott

Regional publications offer enticing prospects for enlarging our personal libraries, enlivening our winter evenings, and extending our cultural horizons—all for free. And just perhaps for treating us to snack suppers or paying part of our rent as well.

In case you haven't guessed it by now, I'm talking about linking the two— the community press and book, theater, and movie reviewing— to make us *reviewers*, not *critics*, which are something else again. We can be purveyors of news about what new books are on the shelves, what new plays on stage, and what new pictures on the screen.

There is space available—and limited amounts of money—for well-written reviews in many community publications. In some cases, the only reason that space remains unfilled is that no one has approached the editor with an offer to fill it with worthwhile copy at moderate or no cost. If we feel confident that we could supply the missing ingredient we may approach the editor with two strong selling points:

1. In any residential community where a local publication is considered viable, there will be an audience for information about books, the stage, and the screen. A timely, intelligent review column will therefore be serving a useful purpose and enhancing the value of the publication to its readers.

2. Book publishers, shops, and theaters aren't big advertisers like supermarkets in community papers, *but* a paper that publishes articles of interest to people who buy books or go to theaters has a readership that interests book publishers, shops, and theaters; consequently, they might become small but regular, and more important, *new* advertisers. We should tell the editor that.

GETTING FREEBIES

Having convinced the editor or publisher that we can help make the publication more interesting to local readers, we can then explain what he must do to help us do our part. We can't be expected to buy books, or run to the library to borrow them, in order to write a review; nor can we be asked to pay for admission to theaters to see plays or movies we want to tell our readers about. But no publisher or theater owner is going to give us books or theater tickets just because we ask for them.

If the editor asks, that's different. Obviously, the *Sunnydale Gazette,* circulation fifteen hundred copies, is not going to publish an equivalent of the sixty-page *New York Times Review of Books.* The space available per issue for book reviews may be as little as a single column, tabloid-size, or a single page in a standard 8½x11 magazine page. It's enough for a review of one book with a strong local interest, by a local author, perhaps, or about a local subject; or for two or three short reviews of special-interest books or talked-about best sellers. At Christmas and other seasons that call for gift giving, a roundup of suitable books with four- or five-line comments would have reader and advertiser interest.

We are the reviewers, and before we go to talk to the editor, we should have in mind the kind of column we want to write and the type of books we want to review.

Later on, when we're established reviewers and the publishers know us by name and may sometimes even suggest a title we would be interested in, we can make our requests directly. Meanwhile, we're better off to let the *Gazette* editor do it, though we write the letter for him on his letterhead. How do we know what books we want, or more importantly, what books our potential readers might want? We read magazines like *Publishers Weekly* (or *Quill and Quire* in Canada). In them we get publishers' advance notices of books. We read the notices carefully, check *PW* reports on book sales, and select a title here and a title there, always with local interest in mind. It need not be by a local or regional author or about a specific local subject. It could be about sailing, for instance, if we live by a lake or in a seaport; or a historical novel about the Civil War if there is a Blue and Grey battlefield nearby. Once books are received, we do our best to write reviews that will interest our readers and attract publishers' attention.

That's enough about getting to be a book reviewer. Suppose we don't like reading books but we love going to the theater or the movies. What we do now is even simpler than writing a letter to a publisher. Armed with an introduction from our editor, we go to the managers of local theaters and movie houses, explain that we'd like to review their shows for our Sunnydale weekly, and request a pair of first-night passes so that we may look at what we want to review. If our serious manner convinces the manager that we're not looking for a free outing, he may agree to give us a try with his next show. We needn't insist on that first-night bit; second night could be just as good if we're writing for a weekly or a monthly magazine. We do need good seats, however, and shouldn't be shunted off into the last-row, corner seats.

It's important that our editors fulfill their agreements to send copies of our reviews to book publishers and theater managers even if our clever comments are not all that effusive.

THE DISCERNING REVIEWER

Reviewing, much as it may be scorned by some defensive professional writers, is a legitimate art. To be good at it, one must have some special knowledge and the ability to discern the difference between quality and trash. And just as a fiction writer must learn *how* to write novels or short stories and a poet to write poetry, we who seek to review the works of writers and playwrights and actors must study the basics of *how* it is done. A genuine interest in the subject of a book and the style of its writer is essential, as are a knowledge and understanding of what makes a good play or a good actor.

We are entitled to report whether or not we found a book, a play, or a movie dull, agreeable, or fascinating—that is our *opinion,* not a criticism. As reviewers, we wouldn't be serving any real purpose if we didn't have opinions, likes, and dislikes, and above all, good judgment. Expressing those opinions through favorable or unfavorable reviews does not mean we are setting ourselves up as critics. Those exalted creatures know all about, and concern themselves with, the *techniques* of writing and performing. As reviewers, on the other hand, we satisfy ourselves and our generally unsophisticated readership if we simply say whether a book or play was worth the fifteen bucks a copy, or seat—and why or why not—and say it in language all our readers will understand.

Now, let's take a look at the three main review categories—books, plays, and movies—and see what their requirements are.

First, the books: Sorry, but it's not enough to say, "I love reading." We're going to be *writers* from now on, not just *readers*. We must find out what constitutes a good review and how one goes about writing it. Part of this we can learn at a writing course or through a correspondence school; it will also be helpful if we study reviews in other publications, not the literary magazines or the newspapers with the big-name critics, but the middle-sized periodicals aiming, much as we will be, at middle-class local audiences.

If the book to be reviewed is fiction, we must be able to give our reader some idea of the plot. Is it a good story? Does it appear genuine, or is it unbelievable? Do we find that the characters bear any resemblance to living human beings, or are they mere dummies or fantasies? Our readers will want to know where the action takes place; whether or not it's good entertainment, suitable for the whole family; if any special knowledge or interest is required in order to enjoy it; and finally, whether it's slow-moving, exciting, ho-hum, or scary.

Getting books to review that are beyond our capacity is unlikely, since we ourselves are choosing the titles. Let's suppose, then, that we've asked for a new book about rabbits, which has just popped up on Smith and Smith's spring list. We know something about them; used to raise them when we were young and lost a small bundle later on when we invested in a chinchilla farm out in North Dakota, only to have the pesky bunnies break out, dash off into the woods, and be devoured by coyotes. The book's called *The ABCs of Rabbitry— Angoras, Bunnies and Chinchillas* (get it?), written by one Peter Hare.

News about the little opus, which sells for $19.95 at the bookstore, will fascinate those of our readers who are rabbit raisers or hunters. But how many of them are included in our particular reading audience? Maybe a hundred. So, to help the kindly publisher who responded to our request and allowed us to add this tiny volume to our library (free), and to please the editor who hired us to do his book review column, we do our best to write a review that will stress the book's universal appeal.

We begin by looking at the record of the author, which, if we're lucky, will be printed on the back flap of the book jacket. There, we may find that he has written about stray cats, horses, and Pekingese puppies. Or maybe he's a famous novelist who took time out to write about rabbits because he likes them. Anyway, what's on the flap will be in our review, and our readers will know that he's not a Johnny-come-lately but an honest-to-goodness professional writer. Here he is, Peter Hare fans, with a brand-new book. That's *news*.

Normally, a three- or four-hundred-word review would cover all that most readers would like to know in a book about rabbits—*unless* the author lives down the street or is married to the daughter of the local Methodist minister. Then the review is not only about the book, it's also about the neighbor who wrote it. As a local story, it's worth maybe a whole column or half a page.

CURTAIN GOING UP!

Now, on to the theater: For longtime theater buffs, and there are hundreds of them in every community, anything that keeps them in touch with the performing arts is welcome. And for people with performing or backstage experience or a record of faithful attendance at theatrical performances, there is a rewarding editorial niche to be filled in the community press.

I know most of us will say that the theater reviewers we all knew about were all great *critics*, not just entertainment-page reporters. We're not aiming at flossy, highbrow criticism that might be used as texts at the Yale Drama School, but down-to-earth reports on whether a show is good, bad, or just lousy; what it's about; who's playing in it; and how hard it is to get tickets.

We're back here in the suburb of Sunnydale, remember, and if we're very lucky, the entertainment editor of the big daily downtown might ask us to do a guest review of a show because he or she read what we wrote in the *Sunnydale Gazette* a while back. Or the regular reviewer for the big-city *Current Events Magazine* might be sick or on vacation, or there might be two openings the same night, and we could get a call as backup. Of such *ifs* and *mights* are budding reviewers' dreams composed.

Meanwhile, and until those lucky breaks occur, we should keep clearly in mind the audience we are writing for. Many of our neighbors like to go to the theater and will even settle for seats at an amateur production by students at the local high school or the Sunnydale Little Theater. They go for an evening's enjoyment, not for a lesson on how to become a Shakespearean actor, but before they shell out five bucks for a seat, they'd like to know: (1) Is the show any good, in our opinion? (2) Is it funny or sad? (3) Who's playing in it, someone they know or a visiting star? (4) How long does it last? Should they take along a snack, or will it all be over before 10 p.m.? They may also be pleased to know whether facilities for the handicapped are provided, whether the seats are comfortable or not, and if there is adequate parking. (These questions may be considered beyond the scope of a theater review, but believe me, in many cases, they are more important than a description of a prima donna's hat.)

If we're good reviewers, answer all the questions a potential audience may ask, and realize that what we are really doing is just what they taught us at journalism school, we're being good *reporters*. We can also win friends by adding a note or two about the theater acoustics, individual performers' voices and accents, and whether or not the play is easy to follow and comprehend (something all modern plays definitely are not. Just look at the puzzled expressions of exiting theatergoers when the final curtain rings down.)

GOLDEN MOVIES, SILVER SCREEN

At last we come to the movie review. How does it differ from the review of live performances on stage? Well, first, more people go to the movies than to plays, and most movies are designed and produced for the masses and not for the elite. We don't write *down to* but should write for a less-informed and less-critical audience. People go to the movies for the story (or the sex and/or violence) more than for the performance. There are a few all-out art-film buffs, but they're not for the likes of us, or more correctly, we're not for the likes of them. Unless, of course, we're one of them and have been members of motion-picture clubs, make our own movies, or are old film fans. In that case, we should be able to find a paper or magazine that caters to cinema addicts and would appreciate an authoritative column by one of them.

Mostly, today's readers of movie reviews are interested in knowing: (1) Is the picture any good? They suspect that every film they see advertised as "the season's biggest hit" is a B movie very thinly disguised. (If there was ever a case of crying wolf once too often, it's in motion-picture advertising. If a good movie does come along, there are no adjectives left to describe it, and no one believes the rehashed ones that are used.) (2) Is the movie violent? How much—too much for those who like their violence in small doses, or too little for those who think an evening's incomplete if there are less than a dozen corpses strewn around the place? (3) How much sex? (In case we want to take our children. The children may not need to be protected against overexposure, but Dad and Mom may.) This topic usually requires a note at the end of the review: "Parental guidance recommended; explicit sex; frontal nudity; heavy profanity." That will almost guarantee a lineup of teenagers halfway around the block before the doors open. And finally (4) What's the word on refreshments? Popcorn have lots of butter? A minor item, we might think, but considered vital information by our younger readers—people under fifty, that is.

Certainly, reviewing books, plays, or movies (and, of course other public exhibitions, art shows, museums, ballet, etc.) is a rewarding alternative to writing our own original books, plays, or scripts. But it should not be looked upon simply as that. It's an occupation that engages the talents of a number of highly professional writers, both full- and part-time. It allows a large measure of originality and self-expression, and it may serve us well in helping us to learn how to write our own compositions better.

The opportunities for those of us who are seriously interested in tackling this specialized field are always likely to be limited to the smaller journals. What's in it for us, except free books and theater passes, the excitement of being part of the world we enjoy, and the chance of meeting new and congenial friends? In most cases, perhaps nothing. Some of the small papers do offer an honorarium of a few bucks a column, not always at the beginning, but later on, if a column catches on and has provable reader appeal. (Don't ask your friends to write letters to the editor saying how much they enjoy your column. Editors know that particular ploy and don't like being pressured. If readers like it, editors will find out all on their own.)

When we've been on the job six months or so, we could do as the country correspondents do, organize a little syndicate of our own. We can send copies of our column to editors of other community papers in our region and tell them they can have it for five or ten dollars a week. Pick up a dozen and we might end up making as much writing informative book, theater, and movie reviews as the neighbor's teenage kid gets for mowing lawns.

But just look at the prestige, and the bookshelf full of books, and the theater and movie passes. What more should we want?

The Seven Laws of Writing

Jean Bryant

1. To write *is an active verb. Thinking is not writing.* Writing is words on paper.
2. *Write passionately. Everyone has loves and hates; even quiet people lead passionate lives.* Creativity follows passion.
3. *Write honestly. Risk nakedness.* Originality equals vulnerability.
4. *Write for fun, for personal value. If you don't enjoy it, why should anyone else?* Pleasure precedes profit.
5. *Write anyway. Ignore discouraging words, internal and external.* Persistence pays off.
6. *Write a lot. Use everything.* Learning comes from your own struggles with words on paper.
7. *Write out of commitment to your ideas, commitment to yourself as a writer.* Trust yourself.

SECTION TWO: MOVING UP THE PROFESSIONAL LADDER

Ten Ways to Get to Know Your Market Better Than Its Editor Does

John Wood

The following strategy enables you to study (and get into the habit of studying) a magazine *before* querying it. If you follow this routine, I guarantee you'll get more positive response from editors because you'll get to know their magazines as well as—or better than—they do.

1. Analysis

Begin by examining yourself and your writing. What's your greatest interest, and what are you most qualified to write about? Are you an outdoor enthusiast, a consumer watchdog, a travel buff? Do you like to write about camping and biking, rip-offs and rights, or cruises and destinations? Narrow your interests and expertise to the bare minimum, and forget the rest.

2. Categorization

Next, determine the *type* of writing you prefer. Do you like features, investigative reporting, humor, essays? Do you prefer doing interviews or roundups? Short pieces or long ones? If you've been writing all over the map, perhaps you're diluting your talent. Editors don't trust decathlete-type writers who do everything well but stand out at nothing. So refocus, solidify, specialize.

3. Selection

Once you've narrowed your field of writing interest, expertise, and type of writing, scan *Writer's Market* for six magazines that best relate to these areas.

4. Conception

Study each magazine's listing in *Writer's Market* and come up with three article ideas apiece—or eighteen total. If you want to alter some ideas slightly to fit more than one magazine, do so. Then put them aside (we'll come back to them later).

5. Acquisition

Find the most recent six issues of magazine #1 at your library.

6. Dissection

Study each issue of magazine #1 from cover to cover—that means from the letters to the editor to the back page. This will be the most time-consuming part of this strategy, but also the most important. Imagine you're the new editor and your first task is to bone up before your first meeting with the publisher. Or imagine you're a consultant who has been hired to recommend ways to improve the magazine's sagging circulation. As you analyze, read each issue section by section (i.e., all six issues' departments first, then all their articles, then all their jokes—and even their ads). Examine all six until you know precisely what the magazine uses (and *never* uses), what its style of writing is, who its readers are, what it wants, and, most of all, *what it needs* that *you* can provide. Then do the same for magazine #2, magazine #3, and so on.

7. Interpretation

By this time, you should see each magazine in a totally different light. Each should be more than just a *Writer's Market* blurb to you now. Several sections should already whet your appetite, and so many ideas will be bubbling up in your mind that you'll have trouble writing them all down.

8. Conception II

So what are you waiting for? Get a pen and go to it. As before, limit your ideas to three per magazine (eighteen total) and feel free to alter them, if desired, to fit more than one magazine.

9. Comparison

Take out the original eighteen ideas you put aside earlier and compare them to the second list of eighteen.

10. Realization

Now imagine you're the editor of each magazine. If you received both lists of queries, which ones would *you* choose? The difference should startle you. In fact, your decision should be as easy for you as it is for a *real* editor.

Choosing the Right Alternative for Your Fiction or Nonfiction

Jean M. Fredette

To most beginning writers, publishing is synonymous with New York, the large publishing houses, and the best-known national magazines. What newcomers to the publishing business don't realize is that there is another large publishing world out there—one less visible, less competitive, no less reputable, and much more receptive to beginners. They are the small, independent presses and literary and little magazines, alternative publishing opportunities for your first article, poem, short story, or book—all types of writing. And of greatest benefit, the editors invite, and even encourage and cultivate, new writers.

Eagerness to take new risks—that's what independent, alternative publishing is all about. Often described as the literary equivalent of off-Broadway, the small presses and little magazines are the innovators and the experimenters in style and subject in fiction, nonfiction, and poetry. Historically, they have introduced new ideas in the publishing industry and set their own standards—or precedents—beyond the whims and dictates of the current trends that govern decisions in the commercial publishing world. Indeed, say these free-spirited editors, "Freedom of the press belongs to those who own the press."

The term *little* generally applies to the editorial staffs, usually skeletal. *Little* almost always refers to payment, too; in some cases, there is no payment at all. But what is sizable is the number of these literary businesses—your choices—about 14,000 small presses and 2,500 literary/little magazines—representing all areas of the United States and Canada in regional publishing pockets surrounding big and small cities.

Little also does not refer to the ideas or themes the small presses and magazines espouse, most often the kind of material the commercial editors are afraid of or confused by: specialized, often offbeat subjects, including antitrend, antinuclear, controversial, even outrageous political, religious, or sexual themes.

SPIRIT DEFINED

Although so many of these magazines and presses are open to first-timers and new ideas and styles, like their commercial counterparts, they do demand *quality* work—as they have in their 100-year-plus history, dating back to the first literary magazine, *The Dial,* which was edited by Ralph Waldo Emerson. Since, Hemingway, Faulkner, T. S. Eliot, Henry James, Kerouac, and many other literary luminaries have published with the small press. Check the magazine mastheads and small-press (book publishers) catalogs today and you'll see, for example, such bylines as Joyce Carol Oates, Alice Munro, John Updike, Philip Roth, André Dubus, and other well-knowns who may prefer to publish in litmags or with the small presses because they know their work will appear in its original length and form, untouched or unaltered because of space problems or conflict of interests, which writers often encounter with the commercial markets. There are hundreds of opportunities for publication for both the top pros and newcomers like you, if you can produce quality work.

For the writer of fiction, particularly serious fiction (the kind of writing the commercial world often ignores), publishing opportunities abound, especially in the short story, short-story-collections, and novella forms. The commercial editors even acknowledge the important role played by the independent book houses and small magazines. They are not just alternatives in fiction [and poetry] to the well-known commercial outlets. According to Frank Conroy of the NEA (National Endowment for the Arts) Literature Program, "they are the mainstream."

A greater number of publishing slots is not the only advantage to alternative publishing. Publication in the small-press world means exposure, a way of establishing your credibility as a writer or helping you find your creative voice. It also means exposure to literary agents and editors of *Harper's, Esquire,* and other magazines, who scan the litmags for fresh talent.

Also on the plus side is the nurturing process of the new writer, a high priority with small-press editors—even in rejections. Personal rejections accompanied by a few encouraging words or a little constructive advice are not uncommon. Dedicated, conscientious, as one editor says, "we work with the devotion and intensity of a Max Perkins or Charles Scribner." Says another, "We provide an intimate and complementary partnership with a lot of give and go"—meaning authors are often able to participate in the editing and production of their book, article, or short story. Generally, there is more emphasis on the individual design or appearance—the extreme care to produce artistically superior magazines or books, some of which are hand-bound collectors' items.

The small press, as opposed to the commercial industry, offers an unlimited range in subjects. Consider the possibilities: For example, quarterlies and journals like the highly reputable *Triquarterly, Epoch, Antaeus;* specialized magazines like *Spitball* (baseball), *Grue* (horror), *Handicap News,* or *Muscadine* (for senior adults). Or magazines on specialized topics such as homesteading, infertility, or survivalism. There are also presses and magazines devoted entirely to a genre or form: science fiction, fantasy, mystery, young adult. The semi-"prozines," small genre magazines, rely on new writers to fill their pages with fiction and nonfiction.

The titles of the magazines or presses frequently define their philosophy or spirit: Peace Press, Challenge Press, Banned Books. The successful New York-based Overlook Press capitalizes nicely on the literary leftovers of their neighbors. Down East and New England Press indicate the area the editors prefer their authors to live in or set their articles or stories in. Thus there should be, quite literally, a magazine or press for every reader—*and* writer.

MARKET STUDY

Because of the vast diversity in subject, size, and submission and publishing policies, you should expect to spend time in your search for the market appropriate to your interests. Before sending off your query or manuscript, it's important to learn as much as possible about the publication or press. A good place to begin your search is with the directories. *Writer's Market* (Writer's Digest Books) lists those (few) litmags or small presses that are well known or pay more than the usual contributor's copies. *Fiction Writer's Market* (Writer's Digest Books) contains all the small, independent markets receptive to freelancers but in fiction only. *The Writer's Handbook* (The Writer, Inc.) is an annual directory of the best paying and nonpaying fiction and nonfiction outlets. But the most complete market directory is *The International Directory of Little Magazines and Small Presses* (Dustbooks), which lists over 4,000 markets, paying and nonpaying, in fiction, nonfiction, and poetry.

Read the listing information very carefully to make the appropriate match for your idea, story, or manuscript. Study the entire listing for subject, style preference, manuscript length, methods of submission—every market differs. Or (per the listing information) you may send for a catalog, writer's guidelines, or a sample copy of the magazine (if the fee is stated). Small-press bookstores in larger towns and cities, as well as college libraries, generally offer a range of small-press books and/or literary/little magazines for your pre-submission study.

GREATER OPTIONS

Before sending off your query or manuscript, be sure to familiarize yourself with the quality and operation of the press or magazine and the publishing arrangement. Because of their very maverick nature, litmags and small presses differ as widely as their interests and philosophies. Some presses pay royalties, others in contributor's copies only; occasionally there's partial subsidy, wherein you pay a fee, a certain percentage of the production. In *vanity publishing*, the author is required to pay for the entire production. It's best to steer clear of subsidy or vanity terms; you may risk losing a lot of money since *rarely* will you get your investment back through royalties from sales. There are numerous alternatives that pay, or at least do not require payment *from*, the author. Generally, littles are low-budget and nonprofit operations. Accept the fact that you're approaching such a market for the experience, the recognition, the opportunity to see your work in print—and not for the financial gain. Regardless, however, you should expect a professional and ethical relationship.

It's also wise to ascertain how old the operation is (usually the established date is in the directory listing) and whether it publishes consistently or only when funds or grants allow. Because of the financial uncertainties in keeping a press or magazine alive, there's a high mortality rate; magazines sometimes go under before the first or second issue. Also, ask about the small-press book publisher's distribution policy. You are eager for publication, but you don't want your books to end up in a warehouse. Asking questions before a publishing agreement (verbal, contract, or handshake) may prevent surprises and disappointments later.

Each small press or little magazine has its own individualized submisssion requirements. Honor their requests and believe the editors if they say something like, "Manuscripts sent without a query will be burned." Like the commercial folks, small-press editors often request a query or proposal before the manuscript. And universal is the return-postage policy. These small enterprises cannot afford the burden of extra postage. Without an SASE (self-addressed, stamped envelope) you may never see your manuscript again.

Small presses and literary/little magazines may not be the outlet or publishing alternative for every manuscript, nor may they be the target for a book, short story, or article rejected by commercial presses and magazines. But there are so many small presses and little magazines publishing alternatives with a variety of tastes and specialized needs, that hardly any writer, assuming he makes a serious effort, can escape getting published.

Stay Home and Write!

Emalene Shepherd

An aspiring nonfiction writer recently told me she is housebound with two children, has no car or access to public transportation, and lives miles from a library. She wondered if she could become a selling writer.

My answer was an unequivocal *yes* because I started selling magazine articles when I was a young mother in an isolated rural area.

Whether you have preschoolers or are a retiree, you can sell articles without leaving home. Your primary source of ideas to write about is logically your family. My parents, husband, son, and even what Dad called shirttail relations have been a never-ending source of themes I've sold to family-type magazines. Some of my articles are: "The Day I Met My Mother" (suggesting we don't appreciate our own parents until we have a child of our own), published in a digest; "Life With a Wife" (a humorous piece), which appeared in a Sunday-newspaper magazine; "Thanks for Coming, Son" (with the theme that we often thank guests for coming to our homes, but fail to praise our family members for being there), which sold to a religious magazine; "Hurrah For The Frozen Pumpkin Pie!" (emphasizing how modern improvements have made life simpler), which appealed to the editor of *Christian Herald*.

Also, ask yourself about the persons you know, "What are they *experts* on?" You can capture their expertise for trade journals as well as home-service and general-interest magazines. Any doctors, lawyers, dentists among them? Any gourmet cooks, nurses, electricians? Anyone you're acquainted with who makes old-fashioned quilts or homemade bread?

Interview them in casual conversation. If possible, don't turn them off by constant note taking, but listen attentively and then write later, out of their sight.

INSPIRATIONAL SOURCES

Nostalgia is "in" for readers of magazines like *Grit, Capper's Weekly, Modern Maturity,* and *The Saturday Evening Post.* Editors of regional magazines and Sunday magazines look for holiday material with strong reader identification related to the past. Even men's and women's magazines use some of this, especially in Christmas issues.

Up-to-date experiences taken from the workaday world sell, too. When I had no experience with computers, but my husband knew about them through his work, I wrote "In-put Leads to Print-out," with the theme, "If our input to ourselves is high quality, our print-out to others can be more meaningful." I used scripture verses to illustrate that each person has to put forth some effort before he can expect results, i.e., he must feed the inner man through study and prayer. I concluded, "We are responsible for our print-out." In other words, it's up to us to use the data that comes our way, work on it, and give back to the world the message that He wants it to hear. The article sold to a religious magazine.

In addition, don't overlook other persons you are able to see outside your family without going far afield. They can be door-to-door evangelists, salespersons, repairpersons, or someone you ask to dinner. Not that you should appear obviously at work. Simply be interested in what's happening in their lives and look upon them as article material.

Many spontaneous interviews have brought me checks from editors. A conversation with an acquaintance about her hearing aid started me thinking of how someone with normal hearing should communicate with one who wears an aid. It sold to a health magazine. A discussion in my living room concerning what it takes to make a second marriage work started me on an article on that theme, and it sold to *Albuquerque Singles Scene.* When someone in my Bible-study group said she could never lead such a study, I tried to inspire readers to do just that in "The Greatest Risk of All." The editor of *Today's Christian Woman* bought it.

IN CARE OF . . .

Someone has said if you're a born writer, you'll be at work even when you're looking out the window.

But no one else needs to know that.

One window affording a view into other persons' lives is your television set. To me, soap operas, old movies, and most variety shows are a waste of time, but depending upon what you're writing about, you might pick up from them historical information, current trends, fads, opinions, and facts related to your subject. You can absorb a wealth of material from many areas through your eyes and ears. By listening to dialogue, you can get hints on how to record authentic-sounding conversation.

Talk shows, news reports, interviews on special topics, and shows of similar format do my homework for me in the nonfiction field. They present new ideas in neat packages, as does *The Muppets* for an original comedic slant on today's world.

Be selective when watching television. Keep a pad and pencil beside your chair, just as you do on your nightstand. Observe, evaluate—be thinking all the time about how you'll later use some of these ideas in an article. Jot down addresses of where you might write for pamphlets or information you might later incorporate into manuscripts.

Another way to be in touch with people is through the mailed questionnaire. If you're unable to travel to interview authorities, you can gather information with this method by following a few simple guidelines.

First, decide whom you'd like to interview. If they are published writers, you can contact them by writing to them in care of the magazines carrying their work or in care of their book publishers. Check *Writer's Market* for addresses. You can find names and addresses of other achievers by checking the latest almanac (*Reader's Digest Almanac and Yearbook* is one that comes out every year in paperback) under appropriate headings, such as "Actors and Actresses," "Science and Inventions," "Space and Astronomy," "Sports and Games." Then you will have a clue as to what card files to check in the library for more information. Your librarian can also help you find experts in various fields and their addresses.

Next, type a list of succinct questions and leave ample space for replies. In a short covering letter, tell the interviewee what subject you're working on, why you're contacting him, your phone number, and your deadline.

HOME STUDY

I give interviewees four weeks to reply because it takes time for a letter to get there, be answered, and be returned. Sometimes, because the recipient is out of town when my letter is delivered, his reply is delayed. That's why I think it's necessary to send out at least a half-dozen questionnaires for a particular article, and more if possible, to include a number of authorities on my subject. I ask permission to quote the person in the final article and offer to send him a copy of the published manuscript, if he wishes, to make him feel confident he won't be misquoted. But, not all writers do this. Your decision depends partly upon whom you're interviewing and the possible ramifications of the topic.

In response to one of my questionnaires for a writer's magazine article,

Ardis Whitman (whose writing I've come across most often in *Reader's Digest,* but who has sold to *Redbook, Woman's Day,* and other magazines) said the most useful thing a beginning writer can do is to keep a journal. She wrote: "Mine, which goes back twenty years, supplies me with a multitude of stories, situations, happenings; and even more important, feelings, responses to situations. Moreover, reread from time to time, these journals give me a sense of the continuity and change which are the thread of one's life and hence, one assumes in a very real way, the thread of all lives.

"Additionally, I clip from the paper and keep particularly poignant stories of individuals who are caught in the kind of situations I write about.

"In addition to mailed questionnaires, a technique I use is the telephone interview for immediate and accurate response. I jot down questions before the call and then note the answers for the kinds of inspirational articles I write; but freelancers who are doing more controversial articles usually tape-record the conversations. After calling the expert, whose name and phone number they have gotten from sources I mentioned earlier, writers will say during the beginning of the conversation something like, 'So that I can make sure I get my facts correct and quote you accurately, may I tape-record our conversation?' The person's agreement recorded on the tape is the writer's legal protection.

"As to dialogue, it is, of course, best to *have* the actual words! What people really say is nearly always more moving than what we make them say. Failing that, nothing beats the time-honored method of saying the dialogue aloud to yourself. Does it sound to you the way people really talk?"

To sum up, then, remember the basic rule of writing: "Write about what you know." That's what you're best at doing. Know yourself first. Next, seek to know others. Then, go to other sources to add weight to your manuscripts, because straight introspection doesn't sell.

Here are my sources of information:

1. *Ordinary people* (By *ordinary,* I mean the ones I see every day.)

2. *Television and radio*

3. *Mail* (Besides sending it out, read everything that comes in: junk mail, pamphlets, flyers, cards, letters, etc.)

4. *Newspapers* (Clip short factual material, quotes, statistics, anecdotes.)

5. *Magazines* (Clip and save not only items that appeal to you, but those that upset you. And don't forget to read the ads.)

6. *Telephone* (Call the library, bookstores, friends, and other outlets for information.)

7. *Interviews* (Conduct them by mail or phone.)

8. *Reference books:*

a. Dictionary (Mine contains more than definitions, including tables of weights and measures, special signs and symbols, pictures of state flags, state flowers, aircraft, and much more.)

b. A synonym-finder or thesaurus

c. Almanac (several come out yearly, and you can order one by mail.)

d. *Guinness Book of World Records*

e. *Bartlett's Familiar Quotations*

f. The Bible (Try different versions. I have *The Living Bible, The Good News, Revised Standard Version, King James,* and *Phillips* translation, plus a concordance. Even if you don't write religious or inspirational articles, you'll be surprised at how many times a quote comes to your mind that has its origin in the Bible.)

g. Government pamphlets (Order by mail.)

h. *Knowing Where to Look, The Ultimate Guide to Research* (Writer's Digest Books. This handbook covers the tools and techniques of research success and where to apply them.)

i. *Writer's Market* (Writer's Digest Books. This directory is a thorough guide to what editors are buying and where to send for their writer's guidelines and copies of their publications.)

As you continue to do the kind of writing you enjoy, you'll automatically collect resource aids that will help you turn out salable manuscripts. Many of them are free. You can drop hints about books or magazines for birthday, Christmas, Easter, and anniversary gifts. My at-home library has grown over the years because relatives and friends know I'd rather have a good book than a box of candy. It's less fattening and lasts longer.

Once you get in touch with yourself, acquainted with the innermost desires and needs of others, knowledgeable about where to get statistics, quotes, and anecdotes without going out of the house, and have studied markets available, all that remains is *to write with specific publications in mind.*

Adela Rogers St. Johns once said in an interview, "It's important to stay at the typewriter. If I go skittering around, letting myself be diverted by other happenings, I'll lose the momentum of the words when they are ready to begin moving."

That "skittering around" is something all writers have to fight. As a rule, if you work at home, you can convince your friends not to bother you during working hours. I work best early in the morning; therefore, most telephone calls are scheduled after 11 a.m. You can't be too rigid about interruptions, but you do have to keep them to a minimum.

One of my cherished clippings from an old *Life* magazine shows Hemingway surrounded by meticulously handwritten columns of his daily word-output: March 22—1113 . . . March 23—1144 . . . March 24—968 . . . And so it went. The winner of both the Pulitzer and Nobel prizes, he was reported to have once told a friend that he had so far put down on paper 63,562 words of his latest book.

We can learn something from Hemingway's work habits. Wishing does not make you a writer. You have to work at it, even to counting every word. Success requires what I once heard Kitty Carlisle say about getting along in life: "Remember that with a soupçon of courage and a little self-discipline, you can make a little talent go a long way."

And you don't have to leave home to do that if you're a writer!

Opportunities for New Playwrights

Peg Kehret

Play writing is fun. What other category of writing allows you to see your characters alive and walking around, speaking the words you decided they should say?

Besides being fun, it's within the capabilities of most beginners. It can also be lucrative, if the playwright is knowledgeable about markets.

Dozens of producers will consider plays by unknown writers. Their productions appear in schools, community theaters, churches, dinner theaters, and colleges. Plays that would never be considered for Broadway production often do extremely well in these smaller markets.

After you have more experience and credits, perhaps you'll be able to write the masterpiece that will dazzle New York and London. For now, though, you should concentrate on producers and publishers who will consider plays by unknown writers. You will find many of them listed in the current edition of *Writer's Market*. Purchase this resource book from a bookstore or order directly from the publisher, Writer's Digest Books.

Your first step should be to contact two or three publishers who buy unagented freelance material and ask for one of their catalogs. If you enclose a dollar for postage, your request will almost surely be granted promptly. These catalogs will contain synopses of all the plays which that publisher is currently offering.

COMEDY OVER DRAMA

The following synopsis of a two-act play, *Charming Billy*, is from the catalog of Contemporary Drama Service: "Volunteer/worker/wife Ruth wants to save an orphaned dog from the pound, but her absent-minded inventor husband, Ned, thinks 'Billy' is a boy. Their teenage daughter misunderstands, too, and blithely announces that her mother is expecting. Hilarious complications result, because Ruth is trying to win an election for a seat on the village council and Ned is trying to promote his flea repellent. The humor is faultless because it builds on character and situation, not just funny lines. An entertaining play for all ages and audiences. Cast: 6 women, 3 men, 1 dog. Playing time: 90 minutes."

Study such synopses carefully, noting subject matter, size of cast, and the markets (school? church?) they're aimed for. This will help you decide what kind of play you would like to write.

Send for a few scripts of the sort that appeal to you and read them. Script prices are listed in the catalogs. Most will range from $1.25 to $3.00 each, depending on length.

Step two is to get some practical theater experience. If you have never attended a live play, by all means do so—several times. Even more important, volunteer to help a local theater group. Work backstage as a props person or assist the stage manager. These activities will teach you more about play writing than anything else you can do. If you can't make time for this much involvement, ask the director for permission to attend a rehearsal or two. Try to attend one of the early rehearsals, when problems arise and are solved. A play is a collaborative effort between playwright, director, and actors. You need to have a feeling for how the actors and director work with a script so that the scripts you write will appeal to them.

When planning your play, remember the producer's budget. Schools, churches, and community groups usually have limited funds. A contemporary play with one simple set that is easy and inexpensive to construct will have more productions than a play with multiple sets and period costumes.

Since there are nearly always more actresses than actors auditioning, you would be wise to write more roles for females than for males. Many times a character can easily be either male or female; in such cases, make it female.

If you can be funny, it's a plus because comedies consistently outsell dramas. Mysteries are popular, too. Again, remember your markets. Colleges and high schools occasionally do a drama, but most of the other amateur markets are more interested in entertainment than in a heavy message.

SELECTIVE SPEECH

Because plays are meant to be seen and heard, not read, your story must be dramatized rather than narrated. The major action should take place on stage. The key word here is *action*. Never have a character standing alone, talking out loud to himself. Unless you are writing an old-fashioned melodrama, your characters should not speak to the audience; they should speak only to each other. If possible, avoid on-stage telephone conversations where the audience hears only half of what's being said. (If you must have a character use the telephone, let his words indicate what the person on the other end of the line is saying.)

Each of the main characters in a play should want something; what he or she wants determines the plot of your play. Let your audience know as soon as possible who the characters are, what their relationship to each other is, and what each of them wants.

The audience needs a central character with whom they can identify. They must care what happens to this character; they must want him to achieve his goal. Give this main character a logical obstacle to overcome, and then put some unexpected complications in his way. If the audience is wondering what's going to happen next, you can be sure no one will leave at intermission.

This external action should have internal results. Your characters must be growing, feeling, changing.

Open your play on the day that is different from the others in the main character's life. It might be when your main character has reached a turning point in her life or when a big decision that will lead to conflict has been made. The audience doesn't want to hear what has already happened; they want to see what's going to happen next. If it's crucial to feed them some past history, do it in a logical fashion.

Never have your characters tell each other something they both already know. For example, a wife would not say to her husband, "My mother, who has been sick all winter, called to say she needs an operation." He knows that her mother's been sick; his wife doesn't have to tell him. Realistically, the wife would say, "Mother called. She needs an operation." If it's crucial for the audience to know that Mother's been sick all winter, the husband could then respond, "She already has more medical bills this winter than she can handle."

How many characters should your play have? As many as necessary to tell the story, and no more. Eliminate anyone who is not essential. You'll need to be more conscious of an excess of characters in adult plays than in those aimed at the educational markets. Students sometimes enjoy bit parts, but most adults don't want to attend weeks of rehearsals only to spend most of each production backstage, waiting for two minutes in the spotlight. Small casts are definitely preferred by producers at professional and semiprofessional theaters. They would much rather issue four paychecks to actors each week than sixteen.

Every line of dialogue must either develop the character or further the plot. Beware of indecisive words such as *well, but, oh,* and *uh*. Such words, especially at the beginning of a line, only detract from the point of the speech. You want your character's speech to sound natural, but art is selective. If you recorded actual speech patterns and used them in your play, the audience would soon be asleep.

BLOCKING

Characters should not call each other by name much, either, once the audience knows who they are.

Use words the audience can understand, or they will quickly lose interest. Plain English is better than dialects or foreign phrases. Keep the speeches short, but be wary of many consecutive pages of dialogue which consist of only one- or two-word speeches; such scenes are difficult to memorize. If you vary the length of the speeches, the actors will appreciate you.

Above all, the dialogue must be *speakable*. Read your play aloud to be sure you haven't written any tongue twisters.

Your play must be more than dialogue; it also should include stage directions. That is, you need to include the characters' actions when you write your script.

Here is a sample which includes both dialogue and actions, from the script of *Spirit!*, published by Pioneer Drama Service. (Arby is an aide at the Happy Hollow Rest Home, where Clara and Esther are residents. David Cranston Tooker is a stuffed cat.)

                          ARBY
We'd better get started on our exercises.

                          CLARA
Must we?

                          ARBY
Come on. It's good for you.
        (SHE stands DOWN RIGHT, with her hands on her hips. CLARA and
        ESTHER come and stand facing her. ESTHER still holds David Cranston
        Tooker.)
Ready? One!
        (Hands on hips.)
Two!
        (Hands out to sides.)
Three!
        (Hands on hips.)
Four!
        (Touches toes.)
Again.
        (SHE repeats the exercise two more times. CLARA attempts to do it but
        she can't begin to touch her toes and she quickly falls behind in the
        rhythm. ESTHER simply stands, smiling, holding the cat in front of her
        and moving its legs in rhythm.)
One! Two! Three! Four! One! Two! Three! Four!

CLARA

That's enough, Arby.
  (SHE sits on cedar chest, out of breath.)
Calisthenics are so boring.

As you can see, the stage directions are in parentheses; the dialogue is not.
Deciding what actions the characters will make is called *blocking* the play.
There are many ways to block a play. Some playwrights diagram the stage and then visualize where each character is. Others use paper dolls and physically move them around so that they can see where each character is at every point. The second method will help you keep track of entrances and exits so that you don't have a character exit on page 5 and suddenly begin speaking on page 8. If a costume change is involved, the character needs adequate time, which must be provided for in the script. Ditto for action that is supposed to be taking place offstage. When a character leaves to attend a meeting, he can't enter again in thirty seconds and talk about what happened at the meeting. No character should ever leave the stage unless the audience knows where he is going and why; otherwise people will quit listening to what's happening while they wonder where your character is going.

PLAY COMPETITIONS

When writing stage directions, remember that *Right* refers to the actor's right as he faces the audience and *Left* is the actor's left. *Up* is the backstage side of the playing area, and *Down* is the front of the stage, closest to the audience. *Stage Center* is exactly what it implies—the middle of the stage. Your study of play scripts and your backstage experience will help you become familiar with this terminology.
    There is a specific format for play manuscripts, and you should use it when you type your play. The sample above is typical; consult the introduction to the section "Scriptwriting/Playwriting" in *Writer's Market* for more details.
    A one-act play usually runs for 20-40 minutes; the script for this length consists of approximately 15-25 manuscript pages. A full-length play typically has a playing time of approximately 90 minutes to two hours (65-100 pages of manuscript). Most full-length plays today are two acts long, although three-act plays are still acceptable, particularly for dinner theaters.
    Your play manuscript should include the following:

1. *A cast list. This should list the cast, in order of their appearance on stage, and give a brief description of each character.*

2. *A description of the set.*

3. *A list of properties, or* props *as they're usually called. Be sure to include*

those that are carried on by your characters during the play.

4. *A list of any special lighting or sound effects. (If you don't need these, eliminate them.)*

5. At-rise *directions. This is a sentence or two explaining what the audience sees on stage as the curtain rises or when the play begins.*

6. *A costume list.*

When your play is finished, go back and read it again, looking for extraneous material that could be cut. Be especially watchful for conversations of small talk that do nothing to further the plot or reveal the characters. If in doubt, leave it out.

When you are completely satisfied with the script, your next goal should be to get it performed. Most publishers will not consider plays unless they have had at least one production. A production assures that a script works as written—or it gives the playwright a chance to make necessary revisions.

Who will produce a new play? One possibility is to enter your manuscript in one of the many play-writing competitions, which are sponsored annually by various organizations. Most of these competitions offer a production as the prize. Many give a cash prize—which is nice, too—in addition to a production. You can learn about play-writing contests from magazines such as *Writer's Digest.* Also, *Writer's Market* contains a listing of contests and awards.

IMAGINATION ON STAGE

Even if your play isn't a winner, there's hope for a production. Community and college theaters will sometimes do workshop productions. These productions will not have costumes or a complete set, and the actors will usually carry scripts rather than memorizing their parts. Workshop productions are often given after only two or three rehearsals, so they aren't polished performances; they are usually open to the public, though, so they give the playwright an opportunity to hear audience reaction. Sometimes, a high school drama class is willing to do a script-in-hand reading of a new work, either for a school assembly or just as a class assignment.

If you can't find a group of actors willing to give your play a read-through, press your friends and relatives into service. They may not read professionally, but at least you'll find out if you have Clarissa speaking on page 80 after she died on page 47.

Many writers wonder how playwrights get paid and what sort of income can be expected. Play writing is a deferred-compensation plan, so if you need bread on the table next week, you'd better write something else. However, if you can wait a year or two to get your paycheck, the rewards can be substantial.

Most publishers work like this: The author receives a percentage, usually 10 percent, of the sale price of each copy of the playbook. Since the playbooks are priced at only $1.25-$3.00, this doesn't amount to much. The money in play writing comes when your play is produced.

When there is a production, the author gets a percentage, normally 50 percent, of the royalty fee. If you collaborate on a musical play, the composer and/or lyricist will share in the royalties.

The royalty on a full-length play for the amateur markets is approximately $25-$35 for each performance. When a group produces your play and gives it every Friday and Saturday night for four weeks, that's eight performances. If the royalty fee is $35, and you get 50 percent of performance royalties, your share from that one production will be $140.

Some publishers will offer to purchase your play outright. If you have a choice between a lump-sum payment and royalties, royalties are usually better. A reasonably popular play in the school or community-theater market will earn its author about $1,000 a year in royalties, and such plays often sell for ten or twenty years or even longer. If you date your play by using current slang or referring to well-known people, you may limit future productions.

You can also send your play directly to various theaters. Some that will consider new manuscripts are listed in the section "Scriptwriting/Playwriting" in *Writer's Market*. If a theater agrees to produce your play, your fees will be negotiated on an individual basis. Sometimes it will be a percentage of the tickets sold; usually it will be a flat rate per performance, approximately the same amount as the normal royalty fee for a published play.

You will get far more productions if your play is published, because then it will be listed in the publisher's catalog.

Play writing has rewards besides financial ones. It allows you to actually see and hear the reaction of the public to your work. When your play is produced, you can hear the audience laugh; you watch them wipe the tears from their cheeks. After all the lonely hours of writing, it is heady business, indeed, to sit in a theater and see the people of your imagination come to life on stage.

Creatively Marketing Your Manuscripts

Rose A. Adkins

Creative marketing—that is, selling a manuscript to a publication that wouldn't ordinarily use that type of article, works especially well when submitting seasonal material.

A seasonal article or story can be twofold: (1) to point out or to bring attention to a specific season (for example: winter, spring, summer, fall; the school season or Easter season); or (2) to provide information about a specific holiday (Mother's Day, Christmas, etc.) that readers already know and enjoy. Sometimes a season can be something people dislike and feel they've had enough of even before it arrives. And that's where creative writers can come to the aid of editors.

The purpose of an article can be to remind readers of a specific season or holiday and its meaning. But your seasonal message can also be inspirational, or uplifting. Yes, to every time there is a season and for every season there is a time (and it's usually at least four months before the editor's issue deadline).

It's actually the slant of a seasonal article or story that gives you the creative marketing angle. Directories like *Writer's Market* list magazines that use seasonal material, but the listings aren't always specific and often leave the word *seasonal* open to creative minds of freelance writers. A seasonal idea is nothing useful without a specific and *new* slant. Creative marketing applies freshness to age-old seasons.

UPLIFT

Seasonal ideas with inspirational themes are popular with many editors because of readers' interest in various holidays and/or seasons that occur throughout the year. Many seasons conjure up a mood or a sentiment that is ideally suited to inserting an inspirational slant into an article. Some seasons in themselves will bring sadness to readers. The Christmas season, for example, has a way of bringing the blues to me wrapped in the first snowfall of each winter season, and I'm usually hit with the mood many times throughout the Christmas season before that holiday finally arrives. So I usually search for inspirational articles hoping to find something uplifting, something that will help guide me through a season that is otherwise not a good one for me personally. Many people are like me—maybe you are, too. By giving an inspirational theme to a seasonal idea, you can widen the marketability of your manuscripts.

One creative-marketing method is to peruse magazines on newsstands. A quick look at the contents page is helpful in providing you with many new ideas and subjects to write about. Better yet, photocopy contents pages from magazines available at the public library. Titles of articles already published can inspire article and story ideas of your own, which you can then develop and slant according to your own marketing choices and possibilities. The best plan for marketing is to check market columns in *Writer's Digest, Working Writer, Byline, The Writer, The Christian Writer,* and other trade magazines. It's also helpful to check the annual index and read back issues that feature articles about writing and marketing seasonal and inspirational material. Although information in market lists in back issues may be outdated, you will find useful hints and ideas for material you can write and submit to other magazines.

Creative marketing is not always without fault, and often the fault may lie with the editors. You'll do well to remember the following three things about editors in general:

1. Editors most often don't know what they want until they see it. It is sometimes difficult to get an editor to describe his or her editorial needs. Beyond nonfiction and fiction general needs, the rest of what makes up a magazine's editorial content is usually left up to writers, their imaginations, and their creative marketing skills.

2. Editors who say they don't use seasonal material will often use a creatively marketed seasonal piece if they are given the opportunity to consider it. This does not mean you can inundate editors with unsuitable material. The seasonal slant must be directed toward the magazine's specific readership.

3. Editors occasionally can use an uplifting article or story for their readers. *Uplifting* can be translated into *inspirational,* and an inspirational article can be used as an evergreen—the kind of article that can be dropped into an issue when space is available. Uplifting articles make readers feel good—about themselves, about the world in which they live and work, about others around them. Themes for uplifting and inspirational articles are countless.

Following are examples of articles—from the basic idea to the completed article developed and slanted for a given audience, then creatively marketed and ultimately published.

POOLED RESEARCH

An article published in the *Cincinnati Post* on Thanksgiving Day, "Thanksgiving Again?", has a subject of general interest. It touches the lives of all people who participate in the Thanksgiving holiday and spirit, and is a simple piece of pure inspirational and *non*original ideas—a sharing everyone can relate to. It is a list of things for which we all are (or should be) thankful. When I say nonoriginal ideas, I'm not trying to be cute—the piece is an old-hat look at Thanksgiving and the traditional things about the holiday. What sold it was the original way in which it was written and marketed. I included local mentions in the piece, knowing it would then be more suitable for the local newspaper market. Had I *not* included regional mention and familiar references, the piece might have been rejected as just another outpouring of Thanksgiving Day tradition. For example, I open with a paragraph about Pilgrim women and the first Thanksgiving Day. Nothing unusual or new about that, right? Then I bring in a personal tone and say that *I'm* thankful for many of the same reasons the Pilgrims were—then list a few other reasons of my own: ". . . Thankful for the 'off' button on the radio, record player, and TV, and for the 'on' buttons for my washing machine and vibrating chair. . . . Thankful for Dick Biondi (a popular local disc jockey) and all the other disc jockeys who help make our world happy!" Throughout the piece, I bring in the Lord's creation: ". . . Thankful for the beautiful colors of the season—*and* lightweight rakes and heavy-duty plastic yard bags." Then I close the article by thanking the Pilgrims for giving us Thanksgiving Day.

Creative marketing also means applying a fresh angle to everyday happenings. When you develop an article and select suitable markets for it, it's much easier if you use familiar and related events—holidays and seasons and happenings that people know, understand, laugh and cry about, do something about, take inspiration and encouragement from. When you write and market an article, write and market it so that readers can move toward better or happier lives after reading it. Let readers feel better about themselves by learning or being reminded that they are not alone.

Another example of a creatively marketed article concerns the subjects of fitness and health. It was coming into wintertime, and I wanted to continue the sun-and-summer fun and exercise I was enjoying at the city recreation park. The park pool would soon be closing for the winter, and I wondered if there might be a swim club in my neighborhood that I could join for the wintertime.

Where were the indoor swimming pools, and which ones offered public memberships? Which memberships were reasonably priced, and what services did the memberships include? I couldn't see the indoor pools, obviously, by driving around town, and the Yellow Pages yielded no specific information. So I decided to find out all I could about local indoor pools and make some money doing the research. I queried the *Cincinnati Enquirer,* suggested how important physical exercise and fitness is to everyone and especially how important it is to continue in winter the swimming that is so readily available in the summer in Cincinnati. My query included a simple prodding question: "I wonder where all the people who crowd the swimming pools in the summer go to swim in the winter? When I find out, would you like to run a service-type article listing all the indoor pools available to the people of Cincinnati?" The editor's answer was an enthusiastic yes. So I did my research, called health clubs, private clubs, hotels, and motels listed in the Yellow Pages, to ask which of these had indoor pools and which offered swim-club memberships to the public. In each case, I interviewed the swim-club director and learned details about the overall services—price, pool size, hours, locker-room facilities, etc. Finished with the research, I turned the piece into a clever service/survey article, which the paper bought and printed along with a great illustration of a dome-covered, indoor swimming pool filled with people enjoying themselves. And through my research, I found a hotel near my home that offered public membership to an indoor swim club.

SEASONALLY APPROPRIATE

That was several years ago. It may just be time to requery on that same idea, which I might do.

Another good thing about creative marketing is that you can remarket a salable idea any time. If an idea, a slant, an article, or a story sold once, it can sell again. Update it, add a couple new quotes or examples and experiences, write a new lead and closing, and you can creatively *remarket* the article—often to the very same market that bought it the first time out.

Humor is one of the easiest kinds of writing to market creatively, humor being the very creative art that it is.

"What's Progress?" is a light, humorous piece that shows the way a family progresses. Originally, it sold to the essay column in *The Enquirer Sunday Magazine.* Creative marketing came into play here because the piece was originally written as a letter to a friend; then I rewrote it for a more general audience. It was reprinted in *Women's Circle Home Cooking.* (Why did I send the piece to that market when it had nothing to do with cooking? I read the market list, which stated that the magazine used humor.) The opening two paragraphs discuss a family event that occurs in our kitchen, with the children and me discussing progress, so I took a chance that the humor and the kitchen experience would click with the editor. It did. Taking chances like that makes it seem as if creative marketing is similar to roulette. It is.

You can write creatively and market creatively. Don't be afraid to try new and unusual ideas and markets. Don't limit yourself. Don't write inspirational articles and submit them only to the usual, known inspirational magazines or religious magazines to which you've been selling. Change your marketing course; work the themes around and practice creative marketing. Submit your ideas and manuscripts to general-interest markets, sports markets, or gardening markets—and remember: For each season there is a time, an idea, a creation process, and an editor.

CHART FOR SEASONAL SUBMISSIONS

There cannot be an article about creative marketing without including advice about the right timing for marketing, especially with regard to the submission of seasonal material. Seasonal material should be allowed at least a four-month-ahead time span. This chart can be clipped and posted above your writing desk. Always remember that, because of production schedules, editors are forced to work on three- and-four-month-ahead editorial schedules (which means they need articles and stories in house, evaluated and decided upon, purchased, edited, and ready to be typeset that many months before issue-publication date). This chart gives monthly deadlines to follow when submitting seasonal and holiday material.

This is a general schedule, but some editors require lead times up to twelve months, and some may require only thirty or sixty days. Check the individual magazine market listings to determine preferred lead times.

CHART FOR SEASONAL SUBMISSIONS

In the month of	Submit manuscripts about
January	Memorial Day, Mother's Day
February	Father's Day, Flag Day
March	Independence Day
April	Friendship Day
May	Labor Day, school season, Grandparents' Day, Jewish New Year, Yom Kippur

June	Halloween, Columbus Day, Sweetest Day, Mother-in-Law's Day
July	Veteran's Day, Thanksgiving
August	Christmas, Hanukkah
September	New Year's Day
October	Ash Wednesday, Presidents' Day
November	St. Patrick's Day
December	Good Friday, Easter, Election Day, April Fool's Day, Passover

Writing the Story of Accomplishment

Helen Hinckley Jones

All of your life you have read stories of accomplishment. Most "tales" fall into this category. Most motion-picture and television scripts do, too. All adventure stories found in men's magazines, as well as many denominational, teen-age, and children's stories are written either tightly or loosely on this same pattern.

A knowledge of the outside size and shape of a story, coupled with sincerity of purpose, can produce not only good, but great stories.

Each story of attainment starts with a goal. This goal may be either good or evil, but the character who struggles toward it is a purposeful person; Ahab, for example, in *Moby Dick*. Where there is a purpose, there is strength.

In order to discuss goals intelligently, we need to take a quick look at psychology. Since our goals are inseparable from the basic psychological needs and urges of human beings, we need to know just what those needs are.

First, there are physiological needs. In order to live, all organisms must have air, water, and food. Many animals, including man, need shelter. Not so apparent as these physiological needs is the need to touch and be touched. Babies institutionalized in the late nineteenth century died for no apparent reason. In more recent times, baby gorillas taken from their mothers have died from no known illness. It is now believed that the lion playing with her cubs, the mother cat lovingly licking her babies, the human mother fondling, patting, stroking her baby, are all instinctively providing this needed touch.

To supply these needs for life itself, man will do anything.

The psychological needs are not usually life-and-death matters, but their being fulfilled means happiness, and the hunger for fulfillment means misery. It is impossible to list these urges in the order of importance, because their order differs from person to person.

Let us translate these basic psychological needs of humans into possible story goals.

The Need to Live

The man who is caught in a rising tide wants to make it safely to land. The skin diver whose air is almost exhausted wants to reach the surface. The hunter who is being charged by a wild boar wants to kill the boar to save himself. The criminal who is being tracked by members of another gang wants to put off the inevitable confrontation. Parents at the bedside of a seriously sick child want to push death back with their bare hands. You could add any number of examples to this list. Call it "I want to live!"

The Need for Love

Most stories, whether presented on the screen or in print, depend somewhat on the man-woman or boy-girl relationship. The need for love is readily seen in these stories. But there are other love stories. The child who longs for a mother's love and the mother who needs the love of her grown children, are examples. This basic need is far deeper than sex or filial love—at least it can be deeper. Actually, the entire New Testament and much of the Old Testament are love stories. The purpose of the central character is to teach everyone to, in Christ's words, "love one another as I have loved you."

The Need to Belong

This urge might be called "I want in!" A boy on the edge of a gang is willing to violate every principle that has previously governed his life in order to become a member. A little scout with heavy glasses never is chosen in any team game. The oldster looks for a place to fit into a world that seemingly has gone on without him. If you have ever needed to belong, you will think of many goals related to this urge.

The Need to Feel Secure

Most human effort is used to get ahead. The man who must succeed in the eyes of his boss in order to provide for his family is an example; so is the number of banks, savings and loan companies, insurance companies, and pawn shops; so is the proliferation of government welfare programs. The government realizes that without security for the poor, there is little security for the country.

All temporal security is not based on money or possessions. A child may feel his world tottering because of his parents' poor relationship.

There is a sense of security that transcends, for many people, physical security. These people want to feel that they are working toward eternal security in a heaven that is far better than earth.

The Need to Think Well of Oneself

Most people have their own set of values. There are things that they will and will not do. "Every man has his price" is only partially true. There is the criminal who won't rat on others, the terrorist who risks his life to destroy what he considers an enemy of the people, the religious martyrs of history. All of these people must be true to themselves.

The Need to be Thought Well Of by Others

The first type of individual that comes to mind when we speak of status is the man who must have the most luxurious house, the biggest boat, the finest car, the most fantastic jewels for his wife, the handsomest children. But there are others who need public approbation. Consider the philanthropist, the volunteer worker in any good cause, the poet, the novelist, the actor. Because we want others to think highly of us, some of us play a role all our lives.

The Need for Something to Look Forward To

It's difficult to even get up in the morning if there is nothing to look forward to. Have you visited an old-folks' home recently? A convalescent or rest home? A mental hospital? A prison?

Wherever life is routinized through necessity, there should be a studied effort on the part of the staff to prepare little surprises, plan for little changes, to vary the monotony of life. We do need the unexpected. Few are the housewives who do not look forward to the coming of the mailman even though the mail is nearly always addressed "Occupant."

If we need these little things, how much more do we need some focus for our hope, our faith, our dreams, our yearnings! Many story goals are based on this need.

Of course the strongest stories are based on the presence of two of these urges in almost equal proportions. The pilot wished to save his life by turning back in a storm; but he has been entrusted with vaccine, shall we say, that is badly needed in an interior village. He must risk his life in order to preserve his own integrity.

Love and any of the others may be in conflict. Shall a person put his own security above the romance of something to look forward to? Note that the real vital choice is between two of the strongest urges. Self-preservation and—you think on from here.

Now to the story you have in mind. What does the central character want? If you have the character well in mind, the answer to this question will be easy. But even more important is the answer to a second question: What does the reader want for this character? For example, he may want to save his life while we want him to save his integrity.

The second answer—what does the reader want for the central character?—is the one that determines the goal in your story. Often, the answer to both questions is the same.

Now visualize the story as a climb toward the goal, a climb filled with obstacles that give the story suspense and drama.

Not too long ago, we were content with this single story line. Now we want to have two levels. It is not enough that a skin diver fights with sharks in order to save a fellow diver who has become helplessly entangled in his equipment. This hero must fight his fear of sharks at the same time as he fights the sharks, which gives him a battle within himself as well as a physical battle. In the double-level story, the top story is ordinarily the objective one; the second story, the subjective.

Today's writers should make a careful study of the stories in popular anthologies and magazines—publications with a high standard of excellence—to find many examples of this sort of story.

Everybody who works toward a worthwhile goal meets with opposition. Some person or some force seems bound to defeat him. He battles against other persons, against the forces of nature, against the weaknesses in himself. We have talked about this battle against the obstacles in life. But in the story of attainment these obstacles are the story.

What will keep your hero from fulfilling his dreams? What will keep him from attaining his goals?

Each conflict must be closely related to the story problem.

There are many ways to write this story of goals attained. Write your story in your own way, but remember that the central character must solve his own problem. If he must be assisted by any outside forces, this force must be part of the story, not a coincidence brought in at the moment that it is needed.

How to Write True-Life Dramas

Don McKinney

Many people think of fiction when they hear the word *story,* but a true story is just as much of a story as a short story is, and often a more compelling one. For example, *McCall's* received a query from a California writer, Paul Bagne, about a young woman who, when she was fourteen years old, had been told that she had leukemia. I still remember how that story began:

> Cindy Walters listened intently to the carefully measured words of Dr. William Lande. "At first it didn't hit me that anything was seriously wrong," she says. "But his voice was shaking and that began to scare me. You know you're in trouble when the doctor is almost in tears."

The doctor went on to tell her that her prognosis was not good unless she was willing to try a radical new combination of drugs that would make her very sick but might help her. She and her parents decided to take the risk, and eventually her disease went into remission. Several years later, Cindy fell in love and married. She wanted a child, but was told that pregnancy—if she were able to get pregnant at all—sometimes caused the disease to return. Cindy did become pregnant, and both she and the baby came through with flying colors.

At *McCall's,* we call such stories human-interest narratives; other editors refer to them as true-life dramas. Whatever they're called, they are accounts of dramatic experiences in the lives of real people. And, like fiction, they are told in narrative form. These stories have always been popular with readers, in part because we all love to get caught up in a good story. And beyond that, such stories often perform a real service. Not only can readers identify with people who have confronted serious problems and overcome them, but also they often can gain hope and courage from someone else's triumph.

We thought the story Bagne wanted to tell sounded like an excellent human-interest narrative, and even though we didn't know him and had never seen any of his writing, we told him to go ahead. *McCall's* is constantly looking for these stories, and we try to run at least one in every issue. Our research tells us that they are invariably among the most popular with our readers, even in issues containing stories of far more importance or interviews with major celebrities. Human-interest stories are also increasingly in demand by a great many other magazines, from *Life* and *Reader's Digest* to most of the women's magazines. They sometimes lead to book contracts and even movie and television sales.

Let me give you a few more examples of the kind of stories I'm talking about, and then I'll give you some hints on where to find them and how to go about writing them.

WHAT KINDS OF STORIES DO YOU LOOK FOR?

Shortly after we had heard from Bagne, we talked to two young reporters from Chicago, Rick Soll and Gene Mustain, about a story they had uncovered for their newspaper. It involved two women. One had severe birth defects and at age three months had been labeled as retarded and placed in a state institution because nobody else wanted her. A few years later an idealistic young nurse came upon this little girl. She found the child bright and inquisitive. The nurse took an interest, fought the indifference, and even hostility, of the institution, and finally succeeded in having the child retested. The little girl was found to be normal, was eventually placed in a foster home, grew up and graduated from high school, married, and had a child of her own. Soll and Mustain wanted to tell us how the nurse and the woman she had rescued had been reunited many years later, and what that meeting had meant to them both.

A writer from North Carolina, Glenn Joyner, came to us with the story of a remarkable woman named Kathleen White who had developed multiple sclerosis and subsequently lost the use of her legs and most of the use of her arms. Then, through a fluke, she saw a doctor's report on her condition. The doctor had concluded that Kathleen was in the terminal stages of her disease and had not long to live. Angry that she had not been told and determined to prove her doctors wrong, she went on a grueling program of exercise and training that not only put her back on her feet, but also enabled her to run in—and finish—a 26.2-mile marathon.

Barbara Raymond, a writer from Buffalo, New York, wrote us about a family named Spiegel, whose youngest child, Annie, had been born with severe facial damage. The Spiegels had raised Annie as normally as possible, but her appearance was shocking to strangers, and as their child grew older, they came to realize that it would become harder and harder to keep her from feeling like a freak. They finally found a surgeon who could help her, and after several operations, Annie was restored to nearly normal appearance.

And just so you don't think that all of these stories involve medical disasters, I should tell you about the writer from a small town in upstate New York, Lorene Hanley Duquin, who wrote to tell us about what happened the previous Christmas in the nearby town of Ripley. A severe snowstorm had hit the area, stranding hundreds of travelers on the highways. The people of Ripley not only rescued these families but also found them places to sleep, fed them, got Christmas presents for them, even found a Santa Claus for the children, and ended up giving them all a Christmas they would never forget.

These writers all had several things in common. They did not live in New York City. We had never met them or even heard of them before. We bought every story, and in each case it was the first sale the writer made to *McCall's*. And human-interest narratives can be an excellent way for you to break into a national magazine, too.

Of course, these markets demand excellence, and the standards for narratives aren't any less than for our other articles. Some of these writers were inexperienced in writing for magazines, and their first tries were pretty rough. But because they had good stories to tell, we wanted very much to have them succeed. We gave them detailed rewrite instructions, talked to them a number of times about their articles, helped them through one and sometimes several rewrites.

Let me emphasize another important point about the stories I've just mentioned: *We did not know about them.* New York editors read the New York papers, and sometimes a few other big-city papers; we read most of the national magazines and we watch television, and when we spot a story we think would work for us, we assign it. Competition for such stories is fierce, and we know from experience that if we don't move quickly, some other magazine will. I can't tell you the number of times we've heard about good stories in other parts of the country and assigned them, often using a New York writer, and have gotten the story in print without ever hearing from a local writer—a writer who might easily have gotten the assignment if he or she had brought it to us.

So, if you live outside the New York area, you have an advantage—you may be able to find out about events and people we will never hear about. But what kinds of stories should you be looking for?

An Extraordinary Experience

Such stories often involve some sort of disaster (fire, flood, earthquake) that places a person in jeopardy. Then they go on to tell how that person pulled through. A woman survives the crash of a light plane. She is badly injured and the pilot is dead. She doesn't know where she is, but she knows she cannot survive long without aid. After waiting several days to see if help will arrive, she starts crawling down the mountain. . . . That was a hell of a story, and we ran it in the magazine a number of years ago.

A Common Problem

This kind of narrative describes how a man or woman or family dealt with the sort of experience many of us have faced or might face, and thus helps us to understand how such problems can be handled, and perhaps how we might behave in similar circumstances. An older couple whose grandchild had been separated from them because of their son's divorce and his former wife's remarriage decided to fight for the right to see the child. They finally went to court—and won. The story of how they were awarded visitation rights has great meaning for others in their situation, as well as being a heartwarming story for everyone. Think of some universal problem and try to find one person or family whose story will make it vivid and alive for the reader.

A National Issue

A few years back, we ran an article about a woman in Alsea, Oregon, who had suffered a miscarriage and found reason to believe that it might have been caused by a chemical herbicide that had been sprayed in her area. Working virtually alone for the next three years, she managed to gather enough evidence to convince authorities to suspend spraying until further studies could be made.

When Love Canal was in all the newspapers, we ran the story of one woman's family and what they had suffered because of the toxic wastes that had been buried near their home. By telling of her children's birth defects, her husband's blinding headaches, and her own serious illness, her story brought this national problem home to our readers. (Incidentally, this was one of those stories that wasn't proposed to us by a writer in the area; we learned of it through the national press and assigned an outside reporter.)

WHERE DO YOU FIND SUCH STORIES?

I asked each of the writers I have mentioned where they found their material, and they offered some pointers that you can use, too. Paul Bagne found out about the young woman who had recovered from leukemia by working as a volunteer for a local branch of the American Cancer Society. "It's good for a writer to stay involved with the world around him," he told me. "That's where the stories are."

Rick Soll and Gene Mustain, the two reporters who told us about the "retarded" child and the nurse who rescued her, found their story by looking through back issues of the newspaper they worked for. One of them came upon a report of a girl who had sued her parents for abandonment, and they were curious to learn the story behind it. They eventually wrote it up for their paper, and later for us.

Barbara Raymond heard about her story on a local TV show. Glenn Joyner discovered Kathleen White and her fight against MS in a newspaper column in a North Carolina paper. "I always check the columns when I'm in a strange town," he says, "because you often find human-interest stories there." Lorene Hanley Duquin, who told our Christmas story, read about Ripley's event in her local paper. She called the town clerk in Ripley and got the details she needed to write her query.

"Finding ideas for true-life dramas is easy," she said in a recent letter. "The newspapers are full of them. Attorneys are another good source—especially if they have a hot court case that is based on some social issue. Once you become established in your community as a freelancer, people come to you with stories. In fact, I just got one the other day. I've met people on vacation that I've done true-life dramas about. And I try to keep in touch with friends and acquaintances who might lead me to a story because of where they work. For example, I have one friend who works in a hospital emergency room, another who is the assistant New York State attorney general in the Buffalo office, and another who is involved in local politics. I've gotten story ideas from all of them."

With a little imagination and a lot of legwork, you can sometimes discover a human-interest story that hasn't been in the papers at all. When we learned, for instance, that new medical techniques were being used to save the lives of premature babies that once would have died, we asked a writer to go to a hospital that used such techniques and see if she could find a couple that had seen their baby saved because of this. She interviewed doctors, talked to a number of couples, and finally found one whose story illustrated the point perfectly. She spent several days with them, recreated their experience, and wove the medical facts into a gripping narrative.

The same approach has been used to illuminate such heartbreaking problems as finding a baby to adopt, or to illustrate the new choices available to infertile women. We have used it to dramatize the new treatments that are saving so many more cancer patients. If there is some dramatic breakthrough in medical knowledge, think about how it might be made even more compelling by using the story of one person or one family as the narrative framework.

HOW DO YOU WRITE THEM?

The narrative form is comparatively easy for the beginning writer because the structure is largely dictated by the facts of the story itself. Every story has a beginning and a middle and an end, and when a writer asks me how to handle a narrative, I usually tell him to begin at the beginning and simply tell what happened—to get out of the way and let the events themselves carry the story along.

The only real decision you have to make is about the lead, because the most effective way to introduce your readers to the story may not be with the first incident in the chain of events you're describing. There is no right lead, of course; no formula I can give you that will guarantee a successful article. But however you choose to begin, remember that your lead has a single, simple purpose—to lure the reader (and this includes the editor, who will decide whether or not the reader gets a chance at it) into your story and to capture that person's interest so that he cannot put it down until he learns how it comes out.

For Maxine Rock, whose story of one woman's fight to save her son from paralysis and death was published in our June 1985 issue, the lead went this way:

> Most of all, Alana Shepherd remembers the blood. It came gushing out of her son's throat when a tube, placed there by doctors because the young man was so paralyzed that he couldn't breathe on his own, slipped out. She recalls a horrible hissing sound, and suddenly the hospital walls were spattered with red. It cascaded over her hair, her face, her chest. Blood puddled in her lap. It shot higher and higher, erupting like an angry volcano. It was the only time, whispers Alana, her hand trembling at the memory, when she really thought her son might die.

From there, Rock went back to the beginning, describing the boy's near-fatal accident, how his mother learned of it, and what happened next.

Soll and Mustain began in the present, years after the drama they were going to describe, with the reunion between Karen and the nurse who rescued her:

> Karen Boldt, a tiny, attractive woman of 32, hesitates a moment, then leaves her crutches in the car. Struggling into the icy wind of a winter day in Detroit, she limps toward a motel coffee shop. Inside, she scans the room until she recognizes an older woman sitting several booths away. Approaching her from behind, she cups her hands over the woman's eyes and kisses her cheek. The woman turns, and they embrace. It is an emotional moment for them both.
>
> Their long and special relationship began 27 years ago in Dixon State School, a cruel and dehumanizing institution in rural Illinois. Karen, left there by her parents when she was three months old, was Dixon's youngest inmate.

Glenn Joyner used a somewhat different technique. Using the marathon itself as his narrative framework, he interwove the current action with the story of Kathleen White's fight to get to the starting line. It began, dramatically, this way:

The Starting Line: It is a brisk Saturday morning in Charlotte, North Carolina, and 1,002 runners are nervously jogging and stretching as they wait for the start of the sixth annual Charlotte Observer Marathon. At exactly 10:01 there is the crack of the starter's pistol, and the pack surges forward. At the very rear, her heart already pounding, is a 35-year-old housewife wearing lavender shorts and shirt and a railroad engineer's cap. Waving to her four excited children along the sidewalk, she appears very ordinary and totally relaxed. She is neither. . . ."

Joyner continued the action for a few more paragraphs, and then cut to give some background:

Kathleen White has been battling with incapacitating illnesses for almost two decades. At the age of 17 she contracted Crohn's disease, an incurable disorder that causes severe abdominal cramps, nausea and chronic diarrhea. But, with remarkable stoicism for a teenager, she accepted her misfortune and vowed not to let it ruin her life. . . ."

Cutting back and forth between the dramatic story of her fight back from paralysis and her agonizing effort to finish the marathon, the first she had ever run, Joyner shaped a compelling narrative. This technique won't work every time—you obviously need some dramatic event to provide the framework—but it's a good one to keep in mind.

After the lead, as you go back to the beginning of your story and relate the events as they unfolded, you must keep in mind that even the most exciting story will not hold an audience unless the characters are human and believable, people the reader will identify with and care about. To make someone come alive on the page, you need details—about appearance, manner, the way he speaks, or the way she moves. You need those little human touches that may do nothing to move your narrative forward but that will make its characters seem real.

Maxine Rock captured these details by talking at length with Alana Shepherd and her son, James, about Alana's struggle to make him walk again after the paralysis. Much of what they told her could not be used in her final story, but only through hours of interviewing did she learn the little details that made the scene she was describing unforgettable. This is Alana's memory of seeing her son for the first time after his accident: ". . . we were in a tiny hospital, staring down at the body of our son. He was too tall for the bed, and his heels were hanging over the end. He looked like a rag doll." Instead of simply saying that he was limp and unconscious, the image of the rag doll said it for her, and in a way that lets readers see it for themselves.

Later in the article, Rock describes the trip back to their home in Atlanta.

It was a long, hard trip. James burned with fever one moment, then turned icy cold the next. When he was awake, his dark eyes were wide with pain and fear;

asleep, he looked ashen and skeletal. James was nearly dead when the plane touched down in Atlanta, but he opened his eyes briefly, and his lips soundlessly formed one word: "Home."

Specific details like this don't just leap at you from the person you are interviewing; they have to be dragged out with lots of questions: "What did he look like?" "What did he say?" "How did you feel?" "What is your most vivid memory of that moment?"

Under Barbara Raymond's patient questioning, Irene Spiegel remembered when her daughter first became aware of her facial deformity. "Annie loved to sing and dance in front of the mirror. One night she stopped, leaned forward and looked at her image. With her fingers, she tried to tug her features into place. 'Why does my eye look like this?' she asked me."

After hours of interviewing Jeanette Cusick, the nurse, about the little "retarded" girl she had rescued, Soll and Mustain were able to recreate a touching scene that took place in Jeanette's home the first night Karen had been out of the institution.

> Karen touched everything—the furniture, the carpeting, the draperies. She was mesmerized by the ordinary comforts of Jeanette's home . . . for the first time, Karen used a fork and drank from something other than a tin cup . . . Later, after soaking in her first bubble bath, Karen snuggled into bed, then gazed intently at the painting hanging in Jeanette's bedroom. Titled, "Love Is Blind," it depicted a little girl hugging a doll. Sawdust tumbled from the doll's broken foot. Jeanette, conscious of how sensitive Karen was about her clubfoot, told her, "When people see your beautiful face, no one will notice your foot."
>
> The next morning Karen opened the first real Christmas presents she had ever received. Among them were a rocking chair and a doll. She examined the doll's perfect legs like a doctor examining a newborn baby. Then she named the doll *Jeanette*."

Talk to your subjects as much as you can, even after you think you have all you will need. I've had writers tell me that sometimes the most revealing comments come after the interview seems to be over, when the recorder or the pad and pencil have been put away and everyone is beginning to relax. Overresearch, overreport, learn much more than you can ever use. Only then will you fully understand the people and events you are writing about, and be able to select the details you need.

A FINAL WORD

Where do you stop? And How? In her story of Alana Shepherd's struggle to help her son recover from paralysis after his accident, Maxine Rock decided to stop with the climax, the moment everyone had been waiting for, even though much has happened to James and his mother since then.

> Doctors insisted on wheeling James to the hospital doors, but James got up, folded the wheelchair and handed it to his father. "I won't need it," he said. He leaned on just a cane and pushed open the hospital doors. Then, triumphantly, he walked out.

Soll and Mustain ended by coming back to the reunion between Jeanette, the nurse, and Karen, the little girl (now 32, with a son of her own) she had rescued from the institution:

> "The whole experience at Dixon," [Karen] says, "was a tragedy. But I try to find good even out of bad experiences. The pregnancy hurt, but I have Michael. I look forward to watching him grow up and accomplish things I couldn't."
> Jeanette tells Karen that's what she always wanted, to watch the girl she rescued grow and become what she is now. "Karen, I loved you from the time I met you, and I love you now."
> "*That*," Karen replies, "is what saved my life."

Lorene Duquin ended her story of Christmas in Ripley, New York, with this lovely image:

> Christmas had come and gone. But the nearly 1,000 visitors did not forget. Cards, letters, and donations poured into Ripley, many from people who had not even been there that night.
> Then, last spring, a man from upstate New York, whose daughter and son-in-law had spent Christmas in Ripley with their children, sent each of the women who had worked in the kitchen three beautiful rosebushes. Now, every June, when the tall shade trees form an arch over Ripley's Main Street, the townspeople will see the blooming Peace roses, and they will remember, too.

Just as there is no one right lead, there is no one right ending. But the ending should leave your readers feeling satisfied, uplifted, moved. Don't simply summarize your story or restate points you have already made, but find some image, some quote, some anecdote that catches the theme of the piece, and by so doing, ties it all together.

It is sometimes said that good stories tell themselves; they don't, but if you have done your job well, they will read that way. You must research the situation thoroughly, talk to a lot of people, find a focus that will hold it all together. Then you must figure out the essential ingredients of your narrative and describe them as simply and honestly and cleanly as you can. Human-interest narratives do take a lot of work, both to find and to write, but they are relatively less complex to put together than a profile or a straight article. They are also in great demand and an excellent way to break into a magazine.

Let me leave you with a thought that will, I hope, inspire you. *McCall's* will publish twelve to fifteen pieces like the ones I have described in the coming year, and if history is any guide, more than half of them will come from writers we have never heard of before.

One of them could be you.

Writing the Juvenile Mystery

Donna Anders

My inspiration for a juvenile mystery story always begins from setting, which I feel is important to mood and suspense. A certain place captures my imagination by telegraphing a mysterious, sinister, or foreboding feeling to me. Later, as I write, I seek to transfer this feeling to my story.

With the setting in mind, I think out the mystery, jotting down clues, or *plants*, which will be dropped into the story as it progresses. However, these plants must be woven unobtrusively into the plot. I select the plants and mystery out of the background. For example, in one of my stories, "Secret of the Silent Mill," which was published in *The Golden Magazine*, I first visualized what could happen in that background. I asked myself many questions like: Why was the mill deserted? Who owned it? My mental gears shifted, and the mystery process accelerated to the supposition stage. Suppose a certain boy's family owned the mill. Suppose an old prospector was secretly panning gold under the mill. Once the mystery seed is planted, it begins to grow into the background. Therefore, it was logical for an old prospector to pan gold in that spot, because the setting was in a mining area. It was also a logging area, which explains the mill. An old wooden water flume, which spanned the creek and was used in helping to resolve the story, was actually a real part of this particular setting. I ask myself questions about the mystery and work out the answers with the help of the background. Although the mystery becomes an inseparable part of the background, it must seem believable that it could happen.

When I have the course of mystery firmly in mind, I then choose an appropriate theme and plot my story from beginning to end. I decide who my main character will be, who my minor characters will be, and the part each will play in my story. Along with solving the mystery, my main character must also solve a personal problem, which is compatible with the theme and other elements of the story.

A REAL SCARE

For example, in my story "Secret of the Silent Mill," the problem was boy (main character) against girl (antagonist); he felt her to be a pest. She was a girl, younger than himself and from the city (opposite character traits). He is a rock collector, knows the types of ore; she is an amateur ballet dancer. The theme was "One should not judge another until he really knows that person." The story opened with the problem—boy and girl in active conflict. The boy was stuck with his younger cousin, who is visiting, and was looking forward to her leaving. Their reaction to a mysterious happening motivated the girl to say something—consistent with her traits and important to the resolution. The boy disagreed, retorted, and the conflict surfaced between them. As the mystery entered the story, the boy and girl became united against the threat (mystery). In solving the mystery together, the boy realized he had indeed judged the girl without really knowing her (theme). Of course, the main character did not come to realize this suddenly at the climax; rather, it was a gradual awareness building toward the final realization. Consequently, in solving the mystery, the personal problem was also solved, thus pointing up the story truth or theme.

As I write, I try to interweave the mystery and problem with the story action. Every ingredient of the story must further the action. For example, not only do the traits of opposing characters motivate their actions and create conflict, but they also serve as factors in solving the mystery.

When the mystery is interwoven skillfully, more suspense is generated, which in turn quickens the pace. I try to build suspense with the main character's sensory perceptions, which enable him to sense things beyond things he sees. These perceptions lead him to intangibles that, together with story plants, add up to the one tangible that aids the main character in solving the mystery.

In the eight- to fourteen-year age group, for which I write, I never have a truly criminal culprit in my story. The threat, or unknown, in the mystery is built up more scary than it actually turns out to be. Although my main character has a real mystery to solve, I do not depend on sensationalism for reader interest and suspense. There are no drastic happenings like dead bodies on scene or supernatural phenomena that cannot be explained later. Rather, I try to build suspense with a tightly plotted, fast-paced story in which the mystery thread is interwoven, not wound around the exterior of the story. I always try to remember that each word must advance the story.

If, at the conclusion of my story, all questions are answered, the problem is resolved, and the mystery is brought into the open and satisfactorily solved, I know that all the ingredients in my juvenile mystery have been added at the right time and in the proper amounts. Then I begin to look for another setting that will trigger my imagination for another mystery story.

A Treasurehouse in Trade Journals

Dennis E. Hensley

I started writing case histories somewhat accidentally in 1967. My father, an optician and ocularist, told me about one of his patients who had "lost" (lodged) a contact lens under her lower eyelid for a year. When the patient's eye was examined and the contact lens was removed, it was crusted with body chemicals. Since I was a college English major, my father asked me to write a brief summary of this case so he could report it to one of the optical trade journals he subscribed to.

As a favor, I wrote the report and sent it with two photographs to *The Dispensing Optician*. A month later—after I had long forgotten about the matter—I received a check for twenty-five dollars and a letter from the editor asking me to send him more case histories.

I was amazed. Back then, I didn't realize that trade and technical magazines *paid* for articles, and I had never heard the phrase *case history.*

I've heard it plenty of times since. I've written hundreds of case histories for magazines in a variety of fields, and in one year I received more than $2,750 for case histories and business articles in the optical field alone.

THE CASE HISTORY OF THE CASE HISTORY

Case histories are 1,000- to 3,500-word articles used by the more than 3,600 trade, technical, and professional publications in this country. A case history demonstrates how a certain person or company solved a problem or learned to handle a specific task in a better way. Most often, case histories explain how to improve quality, same time, please clients, reduce costs, increase profits, or achieve productivity.

The most encouraging aspect of writing this type of article is that you don't have to be an expert in the field you are writing about. You just need to know the basic interview questions to ask and the article format to use.

I have written case histories for insurance magazines, music magazines, and craft and needlework magazines. Working with each type of publication has been a matter of learning the terms and jargon of the business and then interviewing people in that line of work. It's something any writer can do.

For example, when *ShopTalk* magazine made its national debut in late 1983, it was primarily a magazine for black female cosmetologists. Although I am a white male who knew nothing about the beauty-shop business, I found myself listed in the masthead as a contributing editor before the third issue hit the stands—because I was an expert at writing case histories.

Also encouraging is that information for these articles is easy to gather. Nearly everyone you approach in any career field will be willing to talk to you. People and companies enjoy the free publicity they receive from profiles in trade periodicals. Your job is to tell them upfront what you want to discuss and which periodical you hope to sell your article to and then to assure your interviewees that you will allow them to OK your manuscript before you submit it (doing so ensures accuracy for your manuscript and peace of mind for the people you are reporting on; it's important to keep all doors open for future access).

STATING YOUR CASE

When writing a case history, use this basic five-point format:

1: The Grabber. Each case history must have a lead that immediately sells the article to the reader. It should stress benefits (time saved, profits earned, products improved), as in this lead, which I used in an article for *ShopTalk:*

> Louise Michaels, owner of Sunrise Salon in Framton, Ohio, increased her beauty-shop profits by 19 percent last year after training her staff cosmetologists to become effective listeners. "We encourage our patrons to relax and talk about whatever is bothering them," says Louise, "whether it's a spouse who doesn't understand them or a stingy boss who won't give them a raise. Our patrons leave our salon not only looking prettier, but also feeling emotionally unburdened."

This sort of *profits-improved* lead fascinates the reader in the same business, who thinks, If I can learn how she increased her profits, maybe I can do the same. The reader will then finish reading the article. You've hooked him or her.

2: Statistics. Report stats whenever possible, because the reader wants to know by what authority the experts are speaking. A corporate lawyer with twenty-three years' experience will be a more impressive source than a staff worker fresh out of law school. A company executive who has improved production by 17 percent will be more impressive than someone who merely has a theory about improving production.

Important data to include are the names of the people involved and the businesses where they can be contacted. Note the number of years the people have been in this profession or the number of years the company has been in business. You might also include annual sales volume figures, a description of the company's products or services, the number of company plant sites and their locations, and the company's growth rate during the past five or so years.

3: The Challenge. After establishing your source's credentials, state the problem the person or company faced. Usually, it's best to do this in the source's own words, as I did in a recent *Craft and Needlework Age* article:

> "We were really up against a wall," explains Joan Lorell, owner/manager of the Crafty Fox. "We knew that if we used our limited capital resources to expand into ceramics, we might bankrupt the whole business if the new items didn't turn a profit in just four months. Nevertheless, it was our only option if we planned to compete against the new chain store in town."

State the problem succinctly, and explain why it was necessary to face it at that particular time. Setting up the problem in this way allows the reader to speculate as to how he would have handled it.

4: The Conquest. After presenting all the facts to the reader, reveal how the challenge was met. Explain both what *did* work (so the reader can copy it) and what *didn't* work (so the reader can avoid it). Be specific when mentioning experiments, costs, time involved, and how the final results met or surpassed estimates and expectations.

5: Procedure. End the case history with a concise summary of the newly adopted procedure. If new personnel were hired, give their titles and job descriptions. If a new standard operating procedure was adopted, break it down into stages and explain it step by step. For example, I ended a case history for *Insight* this way:

> Gulfshore Optical has benefited greatly from its year of experimenting with substituting press releases for small ads. Says manager Jim Kettler, "We saved ourselves $4,000 in advertising costs, yet maintained our same level of community visibility. Every Monday at the staff meeting we come up with good company-related business news items that can be written as press releases. We've been issu-

ing at least two per week. As long as they keep attracting customers, we'll keep writing them."

Some of the press releases mentioned in the case history were about new products available; others discussed either the addition of new personnel or the promotion of staff members.

CAMERA CASES

Whenever possible, support your manuscript with five to eight black-and-white photos showing people performing the tasks at each stage. Besides shooting your own photos, request company public relations photos from the people you are writing about. If the company's own staff photographer took photos of a development in progress (the construction phases of a new building, the remodeling of a shop, various inhouse training sessions for employees, etc.), ask to review and borrow some of the prints. Also ask for copies of any recent company publications that may contain articles or news items about the case history you are researching.

GETTING DOWN TO CASES

In marketing case histories, follow these procedures:

In your public library, consult *Working Press of the Nation,* volume two—*Magazine Directory*—and volume five—*Internal Publications Directory, Writer's Market,* and *Standard Rates and Data Service—Business Publications*—for information on the variety of trade, technical, and professional publications. Request sample copies of those that interest you.

1. *Ask people in your neighborhood, at your church, at work, or at your social clubs to bring sample copies of the trade journals and company magazines they read.*

2. *Browse the magazine room of a large metropolitan library.*

3. *Request writer's guidelines from those magazines that use case histories.*

4. *Query the editor first; don't attempt to sell a completed case history.*

CASE CLOSED

I will admit that my sales to the dozens of trade and technical journals I've written for over the years have not gained me the same prestige as have my occasional bylines in *Reader's Digest, Success!*, and the *American Bar Association Journal*. Still, my case history sales have kept me busy and added $7,000 to my annual freelance-writing income. And since prestige doesn't pay for groceries, *that's* what I call getting down to cases.

How to Self-Syndicate Your Newspaper Column

James Dulley

For two years, my column *Cut Your Utility Bills* appeared weekly in the *Cincinnati Post*. Like every newspaper columnist, I dreamed of being carried by a major features syndicate. But syndicates prefer to sell columns nationally, and my weekly column on energy and water savings in the home and energy-efficient construction was rejected by all the major syndicates because it lacked national appeal.

But today, my column is read by more than two million people in twenty-five newspapers. In effect, I became a minisyndicate that carries only one column—mine. Like a major features syndicate, I handle the marketing, invoicing, and distribution of individual columns to each newspaper. But unlike the columnists whose work is distributed by syndicates, I share a sales commission with no one.

Self-syndication isn't complicated, but it does require a thorough and detailed marketing plan from the start. After experimenting with several methods, I've found these steps to be the most successful. They can work for you, too.

1. *Select your column topic.*
2. *Sell your column to your local newspaper.*
3. *Establish your column locally.*
4. *Approach major metropolitan newspapers.*

5. *Establish your column in three to five major papers.*

6. *Approach smaller-circulation newspapers.*

7. *Establish your column in at least twenty smaller papers.*

8. *Approach the major metro newspapers again, or approach a major syndicate.*

CREDENTIAL INSURANCE

Before you can syndicate a column, you first must establish the column and land a hometown client. The topic of your column will be a subject in which you are an expert or one in which you can easily establish your expertise. Publish articles in trade journals and become active in local chapters of the appropriate professional societies. Offer to teach continuing-education courses related to your topic at local colleges and high schools. You'll need these credentials when you approach your local newspaper editor.

You'll also need five or six sample columns. As you choose your column format, build in a means to measure reader interest. In each installment of *Cut Your Utility Bills,* I offer free, do-it-yourself instructions, diagrams, and other material to readers who send me a self-addressed, stamped envelope. Question-and-answer columns are also an excellent way to measure interest.

Samples and credentials in hand, arrange a meeting with the appropriate section editor of your local newspaper. Also present samples of your other writing, a résumé, and professional references. Treat this meeting as a job interview, and be prepared to wait several weeks for the editor's decision.

From the start, write and handle your local column as if it were already being distributed to other newspapers. Most newspapers prefer a once-a-week column in the 500- to 600-word range. Include related sketches, diagrams, or charts as needed. (Most papers have an art department that can rework your sketches, so a rough sketch is often adequate.) I mail packets of columns, with an invoice, to my editor at the beginning of each month. I date each column for the week that it should appear. If the paper skips the column for a week, the newspaper is still billed.

Also arrange to have the mail generated by your column sent in care of the newspaper instead of directly to you. I've found that more readers respond to this system—plus, the newspaper editors can see the reader response. (When readers send their questions directly to me, I regularly inform the editor of the quantity.)

Plan on writing only for your local newspaper for at least one year before marketing your column to others. It takes that long to establish your column's success, the readers' interest, and your reliability in meeting deadlines and responding to readers' questions. Work closely with your local editors during this initial period. Their support will help your marketing attempts, and they may provide excellent sales contacts. Someone at one newspaper always seems to know someone at another.

As you begin your self-syndication sales effort, remember that it's both unrealistic and unproductive to mail reams of samples, expecting fifty major newspapers to pick up your column. Set a goal of being carried by three to five major metro newspapers. Look on this first marketing foray as a learning experience, a time to refine your sales technique. If I had approached every newspaper as I did the first several, I'd still be writing for only the *Cincinnati Post*. During the first several months, I revised my presentation materials eight times.

Although direct sales calls are generally considered the best sales technique, it is neither feasible nor effective to travel to the many prospective newspapers. A direct-mail sales approach, on the other hand, makes contacting 200 newspapers economically feasible.

I have found that the most effective and least expensive direct-mail sales approach is the tickle/reply card method. This approach netted me an outstanding 25 percent initial response from managing editors of the target newspapers.

Your only purpose in this first mailing is to tickle an editor's interest and to find the appropriate contact at a newspaper. The direct-mail tickle/reply introduction packet consists of a short cover letter from you, a testimonial letter from the managing editor of your local newspaper, a complimentary reader letter, a reply card requesting your complete samples packet, and a self-addressed, stamped envelope. Don't send any sample columns. Simplicity is the key. The managing editor of a target newspaper should be able to read your entire packet and fill out the reply card (naming the appropriate section editor who should receive your samples) in less than a minute.

Keep in mind that you're at a disadvantage. Many newspaper editors have an aversion to buying columns from freelancers. We tend to be less reliable than major syndicates. And since we usually can't transmit our columns electronically like wire services, someone at the newspaper will have to type the column into the paper's computer typesetting system.

To combat this predisposition against you, develop a professional-looking introduction packet. To your potential clients, that packet is you. Use typeset and printed reply cards and return envelopes. Personalize each cover letter with the editor's name and address.

Develop your mailing list using the *Editor & Publisher International Yearbook* (Editor & Publisher Co., 11 W. 19th Street, New York, NY 10011). It lists newspapers by state and city, and includes a roster of each paper's major editors. Select the names of major papers—200,000 circulation or larger—for your mailing list (but never query more than one paper in the same city). Include any newspaper that is associated with your home paper. The first publication that I syndicated my column to was part of the same newspaper group (Scripps-Howard) as the *Cincinnati Post*.

Address the introduction packet to the managing editor—he can refer your material to the appropriate section editor. Have a complete samples packet ready to mail to papers even before you send out the tickler packet. You can expect 70 percent of those who will respond, to do so within a week, and then it's critical for you to respond quickly, while your name is still fresh in the editor's mind.

In your samples packet, include a detailed cover letter, additional testimonial and complimentary readers' letters, a description of your expertise in your column's subject, other related publication credits, a column as it appeared in your local newspaper, and five to seven sample columns in the form that the newspaper will receive them. These samples should present a broad range of topics within the subject area.

Stress the one major advantage you have over a national syndicate: You can individualize your column for each newspaper. In my *Cut Your Utility Bills* column, I calculate energy savings and costs according to each area's specific utility rates. I also make allowances for seasonal differences, switching from heating-oriented columns to air-conditioning-oriented ones sooner in the Kentucky newspapers than in the Wisconsin publications. Although this personalization requires more effort, it's a major selling point for you. A word processor minimizes the time required for this task.

SUBSTANTIAL RETURNS

Don't mention specific costs in your cover letter. Simply tell the editor you'll be in touch to answer any questions and to discuss the cost.

Make your follow-up call about five days after mailing the packet. If the editor hasn't reviewed the package, call again a week later. Usually, an editor will have a price in mind that fits his budget. You can expect a starting rate of about twenty-five dollars per column from a newspaper with 200,000 circulation. Rates vary considerably depending on region of the country and each newspaper's specific competition. Don't be disappointed if the rate the editor names is much lower than the amount you are paid by your local newspaper—a paper always pays more for locally written material. You can always raise your rate once you prove your column's success. Remember, your goal at this stage of self-syndication is to get established.

Many papers will request a four- to six-column trial period to gauge reader interest. Although I hesitated to accept this arrangement, each newspaper that ran the trial of *Cut Your Utility Bills* ended up buying it. I now offer the free trial but stipulate that if the paper later buys the column, it will be billed for the trial columns also.

Start out each new client newspaper with several columns that drew the strongest reader response in your local newspaper. Then switch over to new columns. Don't try to recycle all your previous columns.

Along with your home paper, these new clients will be the backbone of all future marketing efforts. So *satisfy their needs*. Respond promptly to readers' letters. Even add postage when they've forgotten it. You can't afford to have even one reader call the newspaper with a complaint. Also, keep in contact with your new editors, sending them copies of unusually complimentary readers' letters and telephoning about once a month to make sure they are satisfied with your work. If possible, visit these editors after they've run your column for about two months, after your column has had a chance to prove itself. This is the ideal time to request a testimonial letter from the managing editor. The letter should cover two main points—the strong level of reader interest, and your reliability and professionalism. Don't be shy about saying what you would like the letter to state. If you have handled everything professionally to this point, they'll probably be more than willing to help.

Now you're ready to approach the editors of smaller-circulation newspapers. Your goal is to pick up another twenty to thirty newspapers to gain that truly syndicated status. Be selective in developing your mailing list; I chose newspapers with circulations of 10,000-50,000—small, but large enough to pay a reasonable rate.

Use the same tickle/reply, direct-mail approach as before, but now include additional testimonial letters from your new-client newspapers and readers. You will be pleased with the number of returned reply cards from this mailing— I received more than 25 percent back. Use the same samples packet as before to follow up, except you'll want to add testimonial letters and columns as they appeared in each of the major metro newspapers.

The rates paid by smaller newspapers vary more than among the larger papers. In your follow-up call, openly ask the editor what he pays for columns, and don't let your pride keep you from reaching your goal. Some very small papers pay me as little as six dollars per column. But the six dollars to ten dollars per week from each of my twenty smaller newspapers adds up.

Although the financial return on your marketing effort hasn't been exceptional to this point, you have grown, in a short time, from local freelancer to syndicated newspaper columnist. You're now at a crossroads. You can choose to approach the features syndicates, using your broad-based success as a sales tool, or you can compete with them, adding more major newspapers to your personal syndicate. Either way, you're on the road to professional and financial success.

Are There Hidden Sales in Your Files?

Mansfield Latimer

True, nothing is as powerful as an idea whose time has come, but I have discovered a more important truth: Nothing is as salable as an article or story whose time has come.

I discovered this while filing the copy of an article I had just written. I noticed a short story listed on an adjoining folder: "Second Chance." At the time I had written the story, years earlier, I had thought it was good. But after receiving a dozen rejection slips, I had decided it must not be as good as I had thought—although there were a number of encouraging letters from editors, who had rejected it for various reasons not related to the story. Reluctantly, I had filed it away.

Now, I reread the story, and my faith in it was renewed. Without making any changes, I mailed it to *Columbia*. A month later, the editor sent me a letter that began with the favorite words of all writers: "We have selected your short story, 'Second Chance,' for use in *Columbia*. A check for $300 for the story will be coming to you shortly."

Inspired, I wondered if there might be other stories or articles in my file that could now be sold—even though they had been previously rejected. I discovered a number of manuscripts that I believed could be sold. Most needed a little work—a new title, a new lead, or sometimes a complete rewrite. Working with those stories, I developed a checklist of nine ways to salvage previously unsold articles. Use them to mine gold from *your* files.

NINE KEYS TO SALES

1. Review each article in the light of changing conditions and trends. Is the article now relevant?

For example: I found a short article on insulating a house that I had written long before energy conservation was the urgent concern it is today. I wrote a new lead that emphasized the savings to be gained by insulating. I sold the modernized article to *Rural Georgia Electric Magazine* for twenty-five dollars.

2. Magazines change their editorial policies, so study what is currently being published. A magazine may now be in the market for the type of articles its editors formerly rejected.

For example: Through market study, I noticed that *National Research Bureau* was printing the type of articles the editors had previously rejected. I sent them an article from my file titled "If I'm Smarter Than Joe, Why Didn't I Get the Promotion?," an article the magazine wouldn't have used in the past. This time, the submission brought a check for seventy dollars.

3. Don't hesitate to resubmit an article. The magazine may have a new editor—or the same one may now like your article.

For example: I had written a specialized tennis article that was suitable for a limited number of magazines. I did not know of any new markets and was on the verge of refiling the article when I decided to send it back to some of the magazines that had previously rejected it. It had been a number of years since the original mailing, and some of those magazines had new editors. If the magazine didn't have a new editor, I reasoned that the old editor probably would not remember the article. (After all, it hadn't impressed him on the original mailing.) I mailed the article to *Tennis*. Results: another sale and a check for $200.

4. Sometimes a new title will revive an article.

For example: I once wrote an article I titled "Losers and Winners." It didn't sell. When I pulled it from my file, I realized that the title was negative. Who wants to read about losers? I changed it to the more positive "We Can All Be Winners" and it sold to *High Adventure* for twenty-five dollars.

5. Most writers have received rejection slips with a note reading: "Sorry, but we recently ran a similar article." When you receive such a note, consider it an invitation to submit the article at a later date. The magazine ran that type of article once—chances are it will use another like it. Why not your article?

For example: In a situation like this, following up on my original query to *Office Supervisor's Bulletin* resulted in the eventual sale of "How to Overcome Your Reading Problems" and a check for one hundred dollars.

6. Don't overlook articles that you have sold once. Maybe it's time to update and rewrite. Another sale may result.

For example: I rewrote and updated a previously sold article on marriage, then I sold it to *Family Life Today* for forty-eight dollars.

7. New magazines are being published every month. Study the market section of *Writer's Digest* for information about these new magazines (and changes in old magazines). You may find that some of these new magazines are looking for the type of article you have already written.

For example: *Supermarket Shopper,* a new market for me, bought my previously written and unsold article "You Have Been Ripped Off."

8. As you read magazines and newspapers, be alert for news items that may strengthen articles you have already written.

For example: I recently noticed two separate newspaper articles about dogs killing people. These items reminded me of an article I had written about that subject, so I wrote a new lead that incorporated the stories from the newspaper. *Dog Fancy* magazine bought the freshened story for sixty dollars.

9. Consider the possibility that your article or story didn't sell because it wasn't professionally written. You are now a better writer than you were ten years ago. If the article idea is good, maybe it will sell now if you rewrite it. Remember, you have already done the research.

For example: I rewrote an unsold article about children and money and sent it to *Living With Children.* Results: a sale and a check for fifty-eight dollars.

The process of salvaging salable material from your files is a little like editorial alchemy—turning unsold lead into golden, salable prose. But unlike alchemy of old, no magic is needed. Just some polishing, and some hard work. Mine your files, and find your own gold.

Turning Local into National Magazine Article Sales

Judy Keene

As a beginning freelancer, I followed the same well-worn path toward publication trod by many writers before me—the local and regional markets. *Hoosier Outdoors* bought several camping pieces, and I wrote articles on Indiana people and events for the Sunday magazine sections of the Indianapolis *Star* and the South Bend *Tribune*. Eventually, I began to write in-depth features for *Indianapolis Magazine*.

These publications offered an excellent training ground, but it wasn't long before I yearned to stretch beyond these self-imposed geographical boundaries. I began to query publications in other states, and my list of credits soon grew to include, first, regional publications outside my own area, and then, such markets as *Kiwanis Magazine, The Elks Magazine,* and *American Way.* Although I was now reaching a much wider audience, my articles still were usually based on a local person, organization, or event.

There was still another bridge to cross—the one that would take me to a national audience with a story that was truly national in scope. How gratifying it would be, I fantasized, to pass the magazines displayed at the supermarket checkout and know that my own words were tucked inside, available to literally millions of readers!

At about the same time I had reached this point in my professional life, my personal life was revolving around a friend in the throes of a bitter divorce. She called me constantly, seeking advice and comfort, and I was having a difficult time knowing how to help.

A writer friend of mine recently said that the problem with being a free-lancer was that never again could she just live her life—that every situation was now a potential article. This was exactly the case in my situation. I knew my concern was far from unique and that nearly every woman from Maine to Cali-fornia had been in similar shoes at one time or another. In short, I knew that counseling a friend was an article idea with wide enough appeal for a major na-tional publication.

Some of the techniques I needed now were the same as I had used for the smaller publications. First, I studied the various women's magazines to deter-mine where my idea was most likely to find a home. I listed them in the order that I would query them, putting *Glamour* in the number-one position. Upon analyzing several issues of that magazine, I found that their self-help articles re-lied heavily on anecdotes and professional guidance. This, then, would be the format I would follow—both in my query, and hopefully, in the subsequent article.

I contacted a family counselor in nearby Indianapolis and talked to friends about their experiences with helping a friend through a crisis. From what I learned, I wrote the query.

Within a few days, an editor at *Glamour* called to tell me they did indeed want the article and to give me some basic direction concerning such things as word length. She reminded me that the article must be national in scope and promised that a contract would soon be on its way.

By the time the call ended, I already had visions of newsstands filled with my byline. The writing I now had to do, however, presented some challenges I had never met before; namely, where to find individuals throughout the country who would talk to me about this rather personal subject.

I began by interviewing my local expert at length. She not only answered all my questions on the subject, but she also provided names of her counterparts from West Palm Beach to Lexington to Colorado Springs. These were individu-als well known in their field, and while some were known to her only by reputa-tion, others were friends.

To each person on my list I sent an identical letter describing what I was writing for *Glamour* and explaining how I had gotten the person's name. I wrote that I would be calling their offices the following week, and, should they be willing to help, I would need from their secretaries a time convenient for a tele-phone interview.

All my sources were not only willing, but also anxious, to cooperate. They freely gave me their very valuable time, and not only answered my questions but pointed me toward additional areas I might explore.

To help illustrate the points made by these experts, I needed individuals who had acted as a counselor for a friend. While I had used my friends Karen and Sandy in my query, I felt I would get the best material by talking to strangers—preferably strangers scattered across the United States.

I wrote another letter, once again describing my project, to several friends now living in other states. I asked them to put me in contact with young women who would be willing to share their experiences with me, and once more the response was overwhelmingly positive. A cousin in California led me to her friends, and a college friend now living in Colorado lined up several of her employees to talk to me. Another friend gave me the name of a young minister's wife in Florida whose story was perfect for my lead.

Had this approach not worked, my alternative would have been to use the national directory of Women in Communications, Inc., of which I am a member, to contact fellow members throughout the country. While it was unnecessary to do this for the *Glamour* article, it is an approach I will use in the future. In instances like this one, membership in a professional organization can be a real advantage for a freelancer.

After many phone calls, I had a mountain of notes to transcribe and organize, but my interviewees—none of whom I had known before our conversations—were so open and helpful that the article fell together easily.

The article was mailed a few days prior to my contractual deadline, and during the next several weeks, I was alternately sure the editors were going to be amazed at the manuscript's total perfection and absolutely certain they were going to hate every word.

About six weeks passed before I learned their reaction was somewhere between these two extremes. The editor I had first spoken with called to say the manuscript was "good," but "not yet exactly right." She apologized for her vagueness, but said she really couldn't give me specific directions toward the remedy, although she tried in general terms to explain what was wrong.

For several days, I was at a standstill. Because my writing for smaller publications had always been accepted as it was written, I felt I had been struck a real blow. Who was I kidding, I scolded myself, to think that I could write for the big time? How was I going to face the rejection? And why, oh why, had I mentioned the assignment to so many friends?

Finally, I sat down to the task. I scored my transcribed notes, marking unused material with a crayon and deciding which of it would be included in the revision. I transferred some material from near the end of the manuscript to the beginning, searched for imbalance, scrutinized for inconsistencies. I retyped the manuscript and mailed it, convinced that even if it still was not right, that it was the best I could do.

Happily, the second try was deemed to be "much improved," and within two weeks, the check arrived. A subsequent conversation with the editor at a writer's conference convinced me that four, five, or even six revisions were not uncommon and that I should be proud that only one had been requested. When the article, "When A Friend Needs Your Help," was published in the July 1983

Glamour, I felt I had come to another milestone in my freelancing career. I had crossed the bridge to a major national market, and I had learned to expand a story to make it suitable for a widespread audience. Best of all, I could look at my supermarket newsstand with a new feeling of confidence—I know it will contain my work again!

SECTION THREE: THE BUSINESS OF FREELANCING

Basic Manuscript-Preparation Techniques

Candy Schulman

Throughout our childhood, parents and teachers taught us how to behave, and as adults, we continue to hear their voices inside our heads. Sit up straight, they order. Read next to a bright light, they insist. Never start the day without breakfast. . . . Don't begin a sentence with the word *well*.

Well . . . I slouch. I read in the dark so as not to wake my husband. And this morning, I ate leftover chocolate cake for breakfast. But whenever I slouch over my typewriter, I constantly hear the voice of another taskmaster, one whom I *can't* ignore—my writing teacher. He once filled my head with so many detailed rules that I thought I'd enlisted in the Army—rather than a writing workshop.

Double space, his voice commands. Wide margins. . . . Retype that coffee-stained manuscript. . . . Replace that faded ribbon. . . . Did you enclose SASE? . . . Proofread every manuscript. . . . Hup, two, three, four.

After I made it through boot camp, however, I realized that beginning writers must adhere to certain rules in order to look professional. Be proud of the manuscripts you send to market. After all the work you've poured into them, you *should* be proud. And if you follow some rudimentary guidelines, editors will treat you professionally.

STAGE ONE: BE NEAT

A high school English teacher of mine used to give two separate grades on compositions: one for content, and another for neatness. Editors don't do that. I have never received a rejection letter that read, "Sorry we can't use the enclosed article, but we're giving you an *A* for neatness." Yet, a handsomely presented manuscript puts the editor in a better frame of mind. The same editor might not even read a sloppy manuscript filled with typographical errors, strikeovers, and spelling errors. You're competing with a slew of pros for a busy editor's attention, so you don't want him to think you're an amateur. Editors seek *quality*. Show them your best work in the clearest way possible.

STAGE TWO: MECHANICS

Ready for a tuneup?

Start with a new black ribbon and keys that are as clean as the day the machine was new (use a solvent and a toothbrush or toothpick for those stubbornly clogged *e*'s and *o*'s). If you're using a word processor, make sure it has a letter-quality printer. Editors dislike reading dot-matrix. Inexpensive yellow paper (*copy paper* in the jargon) is fine for early drafts, but splurge on the best paper (white only) for your final copy. After all, this is your manuscript's debut. Paper must measure 8½x11 inches, and the best choice is twenty-pound bond with a 25 percent rag content. Erasable bond smudges and isn't recommended.

Let's start with the title. I prefer separate title pages, with everything centered. A sample:

Manuscript Mechanics:
Basic Manuscript-
Preparation Techniques

by

Candy Schulman
777 Fictitious St.
New York NY 10016

Include your telephone number, but if you live 1,000 miles from the editor's dialing finger, you will most likely get your response in the mail. A word estimate in round figures (2,500, not 2,496, words) is typed in the upper right-hand corner, along with what rights you're selling (ideally, First North American serial rights only).

The first page always begins halfway down, giving the editor room for notes and directions to the typesetter. Every subsequent page follows a standard format. My own blueprint is to type my last name in the left-hand corner, the page number on the right. Some writers include a word from their title next to their names. That word is known as the *slug*. Some writers place all this information in only one of the corners. The upper left-hand corner is most common, though placing the information in the upper right prevents the slug lines from being masked if something is paper-clipped to the manuscript. Which way is correct? All of them. Use whatever method suits you best—as long as placement of the information is consistent throughout the manuscript.

Jump down two to four double spaces and begin the text. Leave at least 1½-inch margins on all sides (some writers prefer about an inch of margin on each side). If your typewriter has a gadget that indicates when to stop at the end of a page, use it. If not, mark the spot with a pencil before inserting the page, and watch for it to appear. Erase those marks later. You can generally fit about twenty-five lines on a single sheet.

Double-space everything, indent five to ten spaces for each new paragraph, and indicate breaks in the manuscript with three double spaces. When you've reached your very last lively word, type *The End* on the next line. Journalists prefer the symbol *30*, which is jargon for *The End*.

Short stories are presented in exactly the same manner. Poems should be typed one to a page; clip longer poems together. Poems can be single- or double-spaced.

Book manuscripts are numbered from beginning to end; don't start numbering over with each chapter. Start each new chapter halfway down the page, and use Roman numerals for chapter titles.

A few words about typewriters: Elite (12 characters per inch) or Pica (10 per inch) are both acceptable. Script type, italic type, and typewriters that type only in capital letters (often used by radio writers) are *not* acceptable.

The self-correcting typewriter is the best innovation, I think, since fire, topped only by word processors, say more and more writers today. But manuals can do the same job, and many writers and editors at the venerable *New Yorker* wouldn't go near plugged-in models, as if they fear electrocution.

Ko-Rec-Type and Liquid Paper, which blot out mistakes so you can type over them, are handy, but a typist who relies less heavily on these products produces cleaner manuscripts. Think about improving your typing, since this skill will be necessary throughout your writing career. When I started writing, I typed sixty words per minute. With practice, my speed has doubled. Should you hire a typist for final drafts? You'll find yourself editing and fine-tuning, even in that last typing. You are better off spending the money on postage and supplies.

STAGE THREE: PROOFREAD
UNTIL YOUR EYES WATER

And then put the manuscript away for a few hours, return to it, and proofread once more. If you're a terrible speller, as I am, check complicated words—even a few *un*complicated ones—in the dictionary. Have you left out any paragraphs from the original text? Check, check, and *recheck*.

You're allowed to make a few neat corrections, but don't let any manuscript page show more than two or three corrected typos.

STAGE FOUR: WRAP IT UP
AND PREPARE FOR LAUNCH

Submit one article or short story at a time. Poetry may be submitted in batches of three to six if the individual poems aren't too long. Using a paper clip (*no staples*), attach the manuscript to a piece of cardboard. A friend of mine used to steal the backs of legal pads from her lawyer husband, but you can buy inexpensive cardboards in art supply stores. I buy stationery and other supplies in bulk from a wholesaler because of a 25 percent savings. And I never have to run out in the rain for one manila envelope.

The SASE syndrome: if you want your manuscript back, enclose a self-addressed, stamped envelope (SASE). A 9x12 SASE fits inside a 9½x12½ outer envelope. SASEs are required unless you're submitting an assigned piece. When mailing a query, use a #9 envelope for the SASE, which fits neatly inside the standard #10 business-size envelope.

Cover letters? If you have publication credits or special qualifications for writing the piece, enclose a brief cover letter. Avoid chatty remarks like, "I've wanted to be a writer since the age of six . . ." Editors are business associates; share your feelings with your friends.

Cover letter or not, direct the manuscript to a specific editor's attention. If I don't have a relationship with a particular magazine editor, I pick a name from the masthead—a nice, sensitive-sounding name. Editors-in-chief are extremely busy, so I opt for a senior or associate editor. Once an editor responds personally, I submit another manuscript quickly with a cover letter thanking him for those thoughtful comments. Relationships develop this way, and so do assignments.

Book manuscripts should be placed loose in ream-sized typing-paper boxes. Enclose return postage and a self-addressed mailing label.

Make sure you have a carbon or photocopy of the final draft. You may think manuscripts don't really get lost. They do, in editor's offices, and in the mail. I'll never forget the tearful woman I once saw in the post office, clutching part of her book manuscript and begging the clerk to find her missing half, while crying, "I don't have another copy!" Don't learn the hard way.

Send your manuscripts first class. Fourth class is cheaper, but slower, too. If you do use fourth class, make sure that the inside SASE and outer envelope both say "Return postage guaranteed."

STAGE FIVE: BLAST OFF!

The manuscripts you launch will often make several orbits and need to be sent back out again. Each time you resubmit a manuscript, it must look fresh. Let the editor believe he's lucky enough to the the *first* prospective buyer—not the hundredth.

But manuscripts get crumpled in the mail. Editors eat your cardboards for lunch. Even though you've stamped DO NOT BEND a dozen times on the SASE, you catch your mail carrier gleefully stuffing it into your tiny mailbox. Must you retype every time?

Yes. And no. Sometimes, I iron manuscripts in order to cut down on retyping. Placing each page between two blank pages, I press it with a warm iron (dressed, of course, in a wrinkled blouse; who has time for *that* kind of ironing?). Then I place the entire manuscript under my unabridged dictionary for a few hours. A new title page and last page will sometimes make the manuscript look new (if the darkness of the ribbon on the two versions matches). But when the manuscript is ripped or soiled, you must retype.

Only a few years ago, photocopies were taboo. Now many editors accept *clean* photocopies. Check in *Writer's Market* first, and make sure your copies are correctly centered, dark, and free from extraneous marks. If you photocopy on 25-percent rag, the finished product looks almost like an original. Be sure to tell the editor that your photocopy is *not* a simultaneous submission.

FINAL STAGE

Put your own voices inside your head until these rules become automatic. You'll even develop a few rules and shortcuts of your own. Whenever you type a manuscript, think about how it will look in print. Make your final draft as close to that image as possible.

And while you're at it, sit up straight, too.

How to Write Query Letters

Maxine Rock

The three basic ways to bring writing to the attention of an editor are the query letter, the proposal, and the complete manuscript. Brief, succinct telephone calls can supplement each method. Proper presentation is an art in itself, and to successfully sell what you write, you must master all three forms.

The *query letter* is the first and most basic form of submission. It is used

1. *to introduce your idea to the editor,*
2. *to give him a sample of your writing style,*
3. *to explain your writing background and your qualifications for doing the piece, and*
4. *to alert the editor to your availability as a writer.*

The query is just that—a question—and the question obviously is, "Do you want to buy a story about this subject from me?" Queries are appropriate either with an editor for whom you've never written, or with an old friend who buys your work regularly but simply needs to see it in writing before he can even give the idea more thought. The only way a query letter for a known editor differs from a letter to an editor you don't know is that when you're writing a query to an editor you know, you can call him "John" instead of "Mr. Smith." And you can eliminate the paragraph detailing your background and qualifications. He already knows about that.

Here's a sample query I wrote to the editor of *Writer's Digest* . It landed an assignment for me:

Dear Bill:

"The great taboo in the South is telling. In a place where it is so important to keep the status quo, the worst thing one can do is tell. And I've told."

What did 45-year-old honey blonde Rosemary Daniell tell? About sex—with both men *and* women. About working with grizzled men on an oil rig, and responding to their lust in that "sweaty, erotic environment." About standing over her mother's body, glad the old lady was dead at last. And about three broken marriages in what she calls the violent South.

Daniell told it all in her poetry volume, *A Sexual Tour of the Deep South*, and in a nonfiction book, *Fatal Flowers*. She's still telling it, in articles for *Playboy* and in an upcoming novel. Her reward is guilt, nightmares about being a snitch, worries when her kids read her work—and the fame and money that comes to a rising star.

Daniell is probably the hottest female writer in the South right now, and maybe the most honest. She talks freely about how hard it is to spill your guts on paper, and how necessary it is for a writer to do it. She's a fussy, deep-reaching researcher, too, and knows how to build a convincing argument for her ideas while she's making readers gasp and giggle over her unladylike revelations.

I'd like to share those revelations with *Writer's Digest* readers with a feature on Rosemary Daniell's personality and writing career. Women writers, especially, will find that her story gives them the courage they need to fulfill the writer's duty: tell it all, no matter how much it hurts.

I'd like to visit Daniell in her Savannah home and let her "tell it all" to me for such an article. Then, I'll write it much as I did the piece on Paul Hemphill for the October 1980 *Writer's Digest*. This time, I think I can get even deeper into some gut-wrenching writer's problems. And I'll come back with good photos, too.

What do you think? I'll look forward to hearing from you.

My article on Rosemary Daniell was published in *Writer's Digest*. I felt pretty sure—right from the beginning—that my query would win the editor's heart. Why? Because I told him exactly what I wanted to do and how I'd do it. I gave a specific focus to the proposed piece; I let him know I'd be writing about the particular writer's problem of telling, and the article wouldn't just be a fluff personality piece on a hotshot author. I targeted the audience, too—women writers. Writer's magazines are eager to address women's specific writing needs. I gave the editor a sample of the style I'd use in the article—words like *snitch* and *lust* and *old lady*. This was going to be an informative yet fun-to-read piece. And I promised photos to boot. What editor could resist?

The manuscript proposal serves the same various functions as a query, but it's longer and more detailed, and it usually lists your proposed research sources. *Glamour* magazine, for example, likes proposals of three to five pages, because the length serves to make the author's intent "crystal clear." And, if you can't come across with a solid explanation of your proposed article or story in three to five pages, the editor *knows* you won't be able to deliver it later.

Proposals start with a statement of purpose, such as, "This article will explore the way author Rosemary Daniell overcomes that particular form of writer's block plaguing many females: 'telling it all.' " After one or two paragraphs of explanation, tell the editor why you want to write the story (it hasn't been done before, it will benefit his particular readers, etc.) and how you intend to accomplish the task (how many interviews, talking to the subject's friends and family, historical research, etc.). You might want to include a sample opening to the article—not just the lead, but also the following paragraphs—to clearly demonstrate your style and ability to write. If appropriate, include a list of about four research sources, such as experts in a particular field, and be sure to let the editor know these sources are readily available to you. If you plan to include photos, maps, charts, or graphs, tell the editor. And, add at least a paragraph of background material on yourself and your specific qualifications for getting the job done right. Along the way, you might also want to suggest a suitable length for the proposed piece, plus a possible deadline date. (You can include such information in a query letter, too.)

The entire proposal is not a mini-article, but a solid outline of intent and an explanation of how the job will be done. Double-space your work and make sure those are neat, good-looking pages; your proposal, like anything else you hand in to an editor, is a clear indication of your professionalism—or lack of it. (For more on constructing a proposal, see "I Have a Proposal," by Bruce Joel Hillman, in the August 1983 issue of *Writer's Digest.)*

Submitting the *full manuscript,* in my opinion, is most suitable for short stories, novels, humor, fillers, and other types of writing marked either by the uniqueness of their presentation or by their brevity. Some editors do want queries for fiction, although most will admit it's hard to grasp the essence of a short story in a business letter. It's also tough trying to write a proposal for a short story, because you're practically finished with the story itself by the time your five pages are full. A proposal is a good way to tell a book editor about your novel, however.

Writer's Market is your first source of information on which of these approaches editors prefer. At the end of each listing, *Writer's Market* notes "Query" or "Send complete ms." The editors usually mean what they say.

Phone calls alone almost never work as a way to present fiction or nonfiction ideas. Editors are visual people; they want to see something in *writing.* Also, it's important for them to get a glimpse of your style on paper before they commit to an assignment. So, unless you do business regularly with an editor and sales can be clinched with a few words over the phone, you'll be asked to write a query letter, proposal, or outline of some sort. The phone call should thus be used sparingly, as a guide to the preparation of your written proposal.

Submitting the full manuscript is your only choice in the case of fiction, humor, and fillers, as mentioned earlier; but the best way to save yourself time, and to make sure you get your article slanted to a particular editor's needs, is to use the query or proposal. Good luck!

Some Reminders about Copyright and Rights

Kirk Polking

Since 1978 when the new Copyright Act went into effect, your copyright exists as soon as you create a work. All you need to do is type the words *copyright 1987* (or whatever year you create the work) and your name on the first page of your manuscript. If you're submitting to foreign markets—say an English-language magazine published in Australia—it would be a good idea to use the small letter *c* in a circle (©) rather than the word *copyright,* since the c-in-a-circle is the international copyright symbol.

Your copyright entitles you to all rights to the manuscript—the power to control that work's reproduction, distribution, and adaptation to other forms. In the case of a story, poem, or article, the law assumes you are selling only one-time rights to that work to a magazine unless you agree otherwise in writing with the publisher. Some magazines buy all rights, so if you think you might later want to adapt your story into a play, or turn your article into a nonfiction book, or collect your poems into an anthology, you don't want to sell all rights to your manuscript.

If you're selling to an American or Canadian magazine, it's best to just sell First North American Serial Rights so that you can retain all other rights for yourself. If you're reselling a manuscript to which you have already sold first rights, then you would offer reprint rights. You would type whatever rights you're offering in the upper right-hand corner of your manuscript. Your copyright credit line could be typed right under that.

If you're making a multiple submission to a number of newspapers with noncompeting circulations, then you could type "Submitted for exclusive use in your circulation area at your regular rates."

Right to Register

If you're making a simultaneous submission to any of those magazines listed in *Writer's Market* or *Fiction Writer's Market* that accept same, you could type "Simultaneous submission to noncompeting publications at your usual rate," in the upper right-hand corner of your manuscript above your copyright line.

Be sure to submit manuscripts to copyrighted publications only. If your work appears in any uncopyrighted publication without your personal copyright credit line, your work falls into the public domain, and anyone can use it without paying you or asking your permission.

One thing to keep in mind: Ideas themselves are not copyrightable—only the specific way in which you present those ideas, such as in the form of a story or poem or article or book, is able to be copyrighted. And remember that lots of writers get similar ideas, so if you send a story or article to a magazine that rejects your query or manuscript and you see the same idea a couple of months later in the same magazine, that doesn't mean they stole your idea. The editor may have already assigned the idea to someone else, or another writer may have reached the editor before you did. You'll often read in the paper that a scientist in Japan and another in California made breakthroughs with certain discoveries at about the same time. The same thing happens to writers.

Since your copyright exists as soon as you create a work, it's not necessary to formally register it with the Copyright Office, unless you think you might have to go to court to prove that it is your work, or if you want to sue someone else for infringing it. Having it formally registered with the Copyright Office allows you to collect damages and attorney's fees if an infringement case is brought to court and settled in your favor.

Such cases are rare, however, and most writers don't spend the money. If a writer sells a short manuscript to a copyrighted publication, the magazine's copyright temporarily protects him in published form, and if he sells a book-length work to a publisher, the publisher copyrights the book in the author's name and registers it with the Copyright Office.

If a writer, however, did have a manuscript he wanted to formally register, following is the procedure: Write: Register of Copyrights, Library of Congress, Washington DC 20559, for an application form for the particular type of manuscript (Form TX in the case of a nondramatic literary work such as an article, story, poem, or book). Fill out the application form and return with ten dollars and one copy (if unpublished) or two copies (if published) of the work to be copyrighted. A collection of works of the same type, such as stories or poems, can be copyrighted as one work for the same ten-dollar fee.

A Writer's Guide to Income Taxes

Scott Edelstein

WHAT THIS CHAPTER CAN DO FOR YOU

This chapter has been written for two kinds of writers: (1) those who have earned (or will earn) small or moderate amounts of money from their writing during the current or previous year, and (2) those who have earned nothing at all from their writing but who have incurred writing-related expenses (office supplies, postage, duplicating, long-distance telephone calls, etc.).

GETTING STARTED

You will need the following forms and schedules to do your taxes: Form 1040 (you may *not* use the 1040-A or the 1040-EZ); Schedule C (Profit or Loss From Business or Profession); Schedule SE (Computation of Social Security Tax); and any appropriate state and local tax forms. You will also need the *instructions* for each of these forms and schedules. In many cases, the instructions are published separately from the forms themselves and are not always sent automatically with the forms, so be sure to order (or otherwise obtain) both the forms and the instructions. Be sure to get at least two copies (preferably more) of each form that you will be using, so that you can practice and make mistakes. I can virtually promise that you will not fill out every form properly on the first try.

    Most beginning writers need only the forms listed above to do their taxes. Most or all of them can be picked up at any IRS office during business hours. In addition, some of the forms are available in banks, libraries, and post offices.

Many libraries also have cassette tapes that give step-by-step instructions for filling out many IRS forms; these tapes can usually be checked out.

Form 1040, the basic income-tax form, determines the total amount of tax you owe or your total refund. Schedule SE computes your social security bill on your self-employment income. Schedule C lists all your business expenses and income for the previous year. Schedule C is the main form of interest to writers and the one I will discuss in most detail. Business deductions (for office supplies, duplicating, etc.) are to be listed on Schedule C.

Before you begin filling out anything, gather all your financial records from the previous year. Make sure that you can follow and understand them completely, that they are in good order, that they are complete, and that whatever you need is within easy reach. Doing this before you begin working on any forms will save you a lot of headaches, and probably some time.

It is obviously quite important to keep complete records of all income earned from your writing during the year, as well as of all writing-related expenses. Income means *any* income from writing—magazine sales, book royalties, speaking fees. Publishers do not make any deductions for taxes or social security from the freelance checks they send you. Generally, it is advisable to keep receipts. Theoretically, you're supposed to keep a receipt of every expense; but if your expenses aren't large, it is usually enough to simply keep a running account for each type of expense (postage, professional services, etc.). You should, however, be sure to get (and save) a receipt for any business expense over twenty-five dollars.

Keeping complete, clear, and accurate records is quite important. If you are, God forbid, ever audited by the IRS, then the better your financial records are, the better your chances are of coming out of the audit unharmed and unruffled.

Remember that any company, institution, publisher, or other source of income that has requested your social security number has already reported its payments to you to the IRS. If a company does send the IRS information about its payments to you, it must also send you either a W-2 form (if you were an employee) or a 1099-MISC form (if you were paid on a freelance basis).

For your own protection, it's important to save all your financial records for five years, and to save copies of all your income-tax returns (federal, state, *and* local) indefinitely. The IRS has been known to question people's taxes years later; state and local tax officials may do the same.

The forms and schedules must be filled out in the following order: Schedule C first, Schedule SE second, and Form 1040 third. After you have completed your federal forms, then move on to your state and local taxes. Information from one completed form is needed to fill out the next form in this sequence.

SCHEDULE C

For most of us, this is the first form to fill out. It is also the most important, as it is where we can give ourselves the biggest legal and ethical tax break.

I'll go through the form from top to bottom. Note that in the standard 1040 book, one copy of the form is marked *YOUR COPY*. Save this copy for your records; the other copy goes to the IRS.

First, the items at the top of the page: For principal business code, write in 8888; under "business name," write your pen name if used; otherwise, write *none*; under "method(s) used to value closing inventory," check nothing and write in *no inventory*. Under "accounting methods," check "Cash." Leave the box for employer identification number blank. Answer no to the question "Was there any change in determining quantities, costs, or valuation between opening and closing inventory?"

Under *Part I: Income*

List all the money you made from your *freelance* writing, editing, lecturing, readings, etc., under "gross receipts or sales" and again under "gross profit" and "gross income." If you made no money at all from your writing, enter a zero in all these spots. Do not list any income from a regular salaried job or from any other activity for which you received a W-2 form (or from which taxes were withheld). All such income does not get listed on Schedule C; it is to be listed only on Form 1040 under "Wages, Salaries, Tips, Etc." Ignore all other lines in Part I.

If you have more than one line of self-employed business activity, you will need to fill out a separate Schedule C for each general area of activity. All writing-related income (including editing, lecturing, consulting, freelance teaching, etc.) can be lumped together on one Schedule C, however.

Under *Part II: Deductions*

This is where you get your tax break. You can deduct *all* your legitimate writing expenses, even if your writing income for the previous year was small or zero. The lower your *net income* from writing (all your writing income minus all your writing expenses), the lower your taxes.

If your expenses exceed your earnings on Schedule C, you have officially taken a business loss. If you show a loss on Schedule C, the amount of your loss should be subtracted from your other (nonwriting) income on Form 1040—leaving you with a smaller total income for the year. Your total Federal income tax is computed from this smaller total income, and your tax thus becomes smaller as well.

Several points must be mentioned here. First, even though most of us write largely or primarily for reasons other than making money, the IRS looks at writing solely and entirely as something done to produce income. For you to claim your writing expenses as legitimate business deductions, then, you must either: (a) make genuine attempts to make money from your writing during the year, or (b) be working on a piece of writing (say, a book or a full-length filmscript) that you intend to attempt to make money from when it is completed. Whether you are genuinely writing *as a money-making activity* is what counts to the IRS. Thus, a poet who submitted his work solely to magazines that did not pay their writers would not be eligible to use Schedule C. (Payment in copies of a publication does not count as payment in the IRS's view.) If, however, publication of his poems in those magazines led to a reading tour or to his earning money by teaching a class, then the expenses incurred in the writing of those poems would probably be deductible on Schedule C. (If you have no intention of making a penny from your writing, but somehow you do make money from it, be assured that the IRS will nevertheless expect its share.

The above example should give you some idea of the flexibility of IRS regulations, and of the variety of ways the regulations can be interpreted.

There is another stipulation to all this: to operate as a genuine business under the new Tax Reform Act, you must make a profit at least three years out of any five.

Regarding specific deductions, you can deduct the cost of any office supplies, postage, and repairs (say, typewriter or office-furniture repairs) necessary for your writing. You can deduct the fees of any professionals you retained for work related to your writing (attorneys, typists, manuscript critics, etc.); any relevant long-distance calls, including tax on those calls; any advertising (including flyers and business cards); business use of your car (either the actual expenses, or if you prefer, a flat rate per mile traveled—see the free IRS Publication 17 or call the IRS for the specific rates and details); and any travel expenses directly connected with your writing (for instance, the cost of hotel, plane fare, meals, taxis, and tips for a trip to New York to see your book publisher). Business meals and entertainment costs, however, are now only 80% deductible under the new law.

Travel expenses are not deductible if you take a trip primarily for pleasure. If you take a trip for both business and pleasure reasons, you can deduct only the business part (i.e., the amount the trip would have cost if you had engaged in only the business activities). If you take a spouse, child, and/or friend with you on a business trip, only your own expenses are deductible.

The cost of commuting to and from a regular job is not deductible; the transportation costs associated with a freelance assignment are.

Sales tax on any business-related purchase is fully deductible as part of the cost of that item.

You can deduct costs for photocopying, duplicating, and printing; dues for membership in professional organizations (Mystery Writers of America, the Writers Guild, etc.); and the costs of books, magazines, newsletters, and other information sources and research materials relevant to your writing.

You can deduct the cost of a class, workshop, or conference if it is *professional* training—that is, training meant to *augment* your skill in an area in which you are already a skilled professional. You *cannot* deduct the cost of *preprofessional* education—education that trains you to *become* a professional. The same course or workshop, then, could be tax deductible for one writer but not for another.

You can deduct the cost of having a professional tax preparer prepare your *business* tax forms—in your case, Schedules C and SE—but *not* your personal tax forms.

All genuinely business-related expenses are normally deductible. This means that the costs associated with hustling freelance-writing jobs (the costs of duplicating and mailing out resumes, for example) are generally 100 percent deductible from your gross income. So are all costs of promoting your book, play, or other project that you yourself have incurred.

If an expense is incurred for both business and personal purposes, you must separate the business and personal expenses as best you can, and you may deduct only the business part. For example, if you buy a new desk for $150 and use it two-thirds of the time for business, you may deduct $100 as a business expense.

The issue of deducting the rent and utilities paid for your workspace can be tricky. If you rent or own a physical space where you do your writing (e.g., an office or studio), then you can simply deduct the entire cost of maintaining that space, including rent, utilities, insurance, phone charges, repairs, and so on. If you use a portion of your home as your workspace, you can take a deduction for it, provided that it is used exclusively for business purposes. If you use it for nonbusiness purposes as well, however, you cannot take *any* deduction for it at all. (This is an exception to the general IRS policy of allowing you to separate a single expense into business and personal parts.)

Here's how to figure your workspace deduction: If you rent your home or apartment, you can deduct the percentage of your total rent and utilities equal to the percentage of square footage your workspace takes up in your home. For example, if your home totals 800 square feet and your office is 150 square feet, then your office takes up 18.75 percent of all your home. You could then deduct as legitimate business expenses 18.75 percent of all your year's rent, utility bills (*excluding* monthly phone charges), and renter's insurance. (Alternatively, if all the rooms in your home are about the same size, you can compare the number of rooms used in your work to the total number in your home.)

If you own your home, the calculations get considerably more complicated—too complicated to go into here. Order Publication 587, *Business Use of Your Home*, from the IRS. A professional taxpayer's assistance may well be useful here.

The costs of repairs, maintenance, and insurance paid on your workspace, either as part of your home or otherwise, are deductible on Schedule C as well.

Your total workspace deduction (including costs of maintenance, utilities, etc.) may not exceed your gross freelance income (your income before expenses) for the year as listed on line 5 of Schedule C. For example, if your workspace cost you $700 to maintain last year but you took in only $500 from your writing, you can deduct only $500 for the cost of your workspace.

If you have a separate phone line for your business or workspace, you can, of course, deduct the entire cost of phone service for that line. However, if you use a phone for both business and personal purposes, you may *not* deduct *any* portion of the cost of telephone service as a business expense, *even if* you have a separate workspace in your home. (However, the cost of long-distance business calls is, of course, deductible.)

If you purchase office furniture, a typewriter, a computer, or any other expensive item that will last more than a year, you can either (a) deduct the entire cost of the item as a one-time business expense; or, if you prefer, (b) deduct a part of the cost of the item each year over a five-year period. You may, of course, in the same year choose one option for some items and the other option for others. It all depends on how much you want to reduce your taxes this year and how much you want to reduce your taxes in the years to come. In both the cases of one-time deductions and five-year deductions, you must use Form 4562 (Depreciation and Amortization).

The five-year deduction method is called *depreciation* in IRS terminology. The total of all depreciation deductions gets listed in Part II of Schedule C; itemized depreciations must be listed on Form 4562 also. The IRS has its own special formula that you must use for figuring depreciation; you cannot simply deduct one-fifth of the cost each year, but 15 percent the first year, 22 percent the second year, and 21 percent for each of the next three years. You will need to make allowances for items purchased or otherwise brought into service in the middle of the year. If an item is used for both business and personal purposes, you can depreciate only the business part (i.e., a percentage of the cost equal to the percentage of the item's use that is business-oriented).

To complete Schedule C, answer no to the question, "Do you have amounts for which you are not at risk in this business?" Total your deductions and subtract the sum from your gross income; the result is your net profit or loss. If your deductions exceed your gross income, then your net loss should be listed as a negative number.

Ignore the section of Schedule C entitled "Cost of Goods Sold and/or Operations." Leave this section blank.

On the *reverse* side of Schedule C, in the lower right, write *Freelance Writer* in the appropriate spot.

Now go back and *triple-check* all your figures. If they all seem correct, you are done with Schedule C.

Your profit or loss listed on Schedule C should now be listed on line 2 of Schedule SE and on line 12 of your Form 1040. If you have filled out more than one Schedule C (for more than one general area of business activity), add up all your net profits and/or losses and put this total on the lines indicated above.

For more information on Schedule C, order IRS Publication 535, *Business Expenses*. Publication 374, *Tax Guide for Small Businesses*, may also be helpful.

SCHEDULE SE

When you have properly filled out Schedule C and triple-checked to make sure everything about it is correct, you are ready to move on to Schedule SE, Computation of Social Security Self-Employment Tax. This tax must be paid to the federal government in addition to your Federal income tax.

Two copies of this schedule appear in the standard 1040 book. One copy, marked *YOUR COPY*, appears on the back of your copy of Schedule C. Keep this copy for your records; send the other to the IRS.

If you are someone else's employee, social security (FICA) is automatically withheld from your paychecks. But if you are self-employed, either partly or entirely, you must pay social security tax on all your self-employment income. Schedule SE will determine exactly how much FICA you owe.

Schedule SE is fairly straightforward and simple, and the printed instructions should tell you everything you need to know. For most writers, it is a simple matter of taking your total profit (net income) from Schedule C and multiplying it by the percentage the IRS gives you on Schedule SE. The result is your social security tax on your self-employment income.

Note: If your income from writing (after deductions) is less than $400, you do not have to pay any social security tax on this income or file Schedule SE. If you show a loss for your writing for the year, you, of course, pay no social security tax. However, although a loss on Schedule C can reduce your *Federal income tax* on your nonwriting income, it *cannot* entitle you to a refund of any *social security tax* withheld from your salary during the previous year. That is, once any social security tax has been withheld from your salary, it is gone from your hands forever. The best Schedule SE can do for you is to reduce your *additional* social security tax to zero.

FORM 1040

After you're done with Schedule SE, you've come to the last leg: Form 1040. Form 1040 determines the final amount you owe the IRS (or the IRS owes you). It takes into account both federal income tax and social security tax.

You can very likely fill out the 1040 using only the IRS's instructions as your guide—but do so slowly and carefully. It may take a couple of tries (and several torn-up forms) before you get it filled out correctly. Don't forget to deduct the personal exemption ($1,900 in 1987) for each dependent, including yourself, from your total income. Also be sure to triple-check that every figure is correct and in the proper place; triple-check your math, too.

ESTIMATED TAX

If you work for someone else, Federal income tax, social security, and state and local income taxes are normally withheld from your salary. If you are self-employed, however, and your self-employment earnings are more than minimal, then you must do your own withholding from this income. This is called estimated tax.

If you expect a significant portion of your total income for the *current* year to be earned through self-employment (either from your writing, from non-writing sources, or both), then you may have to file and pay estimated tax.

Basically, for filing estimated tax, you estimate in advance what your total income for the year will be. Then you figure out what your total Federal taxes (both Federal income tax and social security) will be on that income. Then you determine how much of your total tax, if any, will be withheld during the year by employers. The taxes you expect you will owe over and above those withheld by employers should be paid as estimated tax. This amount gets split into four quarterly payments.

Most states expect you to do the same thing with your state taxes, and most have the same procedures and deadlines as the IRS. Most cities and counties that levy personal income taxes also have similar procedures and deadlines. Each state, city, and county will have its own estimated tax forms which you are required to use.

For your Federal estimated tax, file Form 1040-ES quarterly, by the following dates: April 15, June 15, September 15, and January 15 (of the following year). These are the dates by which your returns must be *postmarked*.

You are expected to make each of your estimated tax payments (roughly one-quarter of your total estimated tax bill for the year) at the same time you file. Fortunately, Form 1040-ES is very easy to fill out: you simply list the amount of money you are enclosing, and send it along with your check. You are supposed to go through a *very* complicated process to figure out how much to send—but for most freelancers, whose income depends largely on the unpredictable judgments (and even the caprice) of editors, and which therefore can be very variable, I recommend simply making your best and most honest guess. If you make more or less money in any quarter than you expected, you can simply send in a larger or smaller estimated tax payment.

The matter of how much you must earn from writing before you are required to pay estimated tax is a tad tricky. The IRS says that you should pay estimated tax if such tax will total more than $500, or if the amount of taxes (both Federal tax and social security) withheld from your salary will equal less than 80% of your total Federal and social security tax bill for that year.

If you make quarterly estimated tax payments and file four Form 1040-ES's, you must still file Form 1040 (including Schedules C and SE) between January 1 and April 15, just like everyone else. This means that between January 1 and April 15 of each year, you must file *three* sets of tax returns: the standard Form 1040, covering the previous tax year, plus Schedules C and SE; and two Form 1040-ESs, one due by January 15, and one due by April 15.

Failure to pay all or part of the required estimated tax usually results in a penalty, currently computed at the annual rate of 10% of the underpaid tax. However, the penalty will not be levied against you if the total of all four estimated tax payments and all the taxes withheld by the Federal government from your salary during the year equals 80% or more of your actual tax owed. Nor will it be levied if the total of all four estimated tax payments and all taxes withheld from your salary by the Federal government during the year is equal to or more than the combined amount of Federal income and social security taxes you actually paid during the *previous* tax year.

When you make each estimated tax payment, write your social security number and the words "1040-ES" on your check or money order.

STATE AND LOCAL TAXES

For the most part, your state and local taxes are determined by the figures on your Federal income tax forms, particularly Form 1040.

However, each state and locality has its own unique tax regulations, forms, and procedures; these not only differ, sometimes widely, from state to state and from locality to locality, but they also often differ widely from *Federal* regulations, forms, and procedures. Some states and localities tax certain kinds of income that the IRS does not, and vice versa; some states' and localities' rules regarding deductions differ from those of the Federal government.

Filing a form with the IRS has no effect on your state or locality, and vice versa. You must deal with the state and local tax people as separate entities. You will need to file the proper state and local tax forms in the manners and by the deadlines required by your state and locality.

Most states require, as part of your state tax return, a photocopy of your entire Federal return, including Schedules C and SE, Form 1040, and all other forms and schedules that you included. Normally, your local tax return should include these same items.

SOME FINAL WORDS

When you're done filling out all your forms, be sure to check everything three more times to make certain it's all correct. Then sign and date *every* necessary form everywhere you're supposed to (and check to make sure you've done this). Make sure your social security number is on every form in the proper spot. Make photocopies of all the forms (Federal, state, *and* local) for your own records (and save them), and then mail everything. If you owe money, be sure you've enclosed a signed check or money order, and be sure your social security number and the words *Form 1040* appear on it. This is true for your state and local returns as well.

Normally, your return must be postmarked no later than April 15. If this date (or any other date on which a form is due) falls on a Saturday, Sunday, or Federal holiday, your return must be postmarked by the next business day.

If you are entitled to a refund and it has not arrived ten weeks after you filed your tax forms, you may call a special IRS number to have the status of your refund checked. See the section on Tele-Tax in the back of the standard 1040 booklet, or call the IRS, for details.

If you need clarification of anything in this chapter, I urge you to contact the IRS or a professional tax preparer.

Contributors to This Book

Rose A. Adkins

Rose A. Adkins has been a writer and editor for more than thirty years. She was associate editor of *Writer's Digest* from 1975 to 1984 and editor of *Writer's Market* from 1971 to 1975. Her articles, stories, and poetry have been published in numerous magazines and newspapers. She is co-author of *Writing for Religious and Other Specialty Markets* (Broadman) and co-editor of *The Beginning Writer's Answer Book* (Writer's Digest Books).

Ludmilla Alexander

Ludmilla Alexander is a freelance writer, based in Saratoga, California. A former staff writer for *Parents' Magazine* in New York City, she specializes in travel and general interest articles. Her work has appeared in a number of California newspapers, magazines and trade publications. Nationally, she has published in *Writer's Digest*, *Lady's Circle*, *Editor & Publisher*, and (for young readers) *Cricket* and *Young Miss*.

Donna Anders

Donna Anders has sold hundreds of short stories, articles, poems, and short plays. She has two picture/coloring books to her credit and three novels, the most recent having been published by Bantam Books in 1986. An instructor for the Writer's Digest School, she also teaches at local colleges and is a frequent speaker at West Coast writers' conferences. She is working on her third historical saga.

Bim Angst

Bim Angst is assistant to the publisher at *MidWeeker*, a weekly newspaper in central eastern Pennsylvania with a circulation of 29,500. Her articles have been published in *American Baby*, *Modern Bride*, and other magazines, and her poetry, fiction, and plays have been widely published in literary magazines. She's been the recipient of a Creative Writing Fellowship from the National Endowment for the Arts and a residency at Yaddo.

Louise Boggess

Louise Boggess earned her B.A., M.A., and Phi Beta Kappa from the University of Texas. When her husband's work moved them to San Francisco, she taught professional writing at San Mateo College by classroom, television, and now video cassette. She teaches correspondence writing courses for the University of California/Berkeley and for Writer's Digest School. Mrs. Boggess has become nationally known for her three books on how-to write and two on American cut glass, co-authored with her husband, Bill. Published in numerous magazines, she has been a staff member of fifty writers' conferences.

Jean Bryant

Jean Bryant had always devoured books—sometimes at the rate of seven a day. But she decided just being a passive reader wasn't satisfying enough, so she enrolled in a writing class. A few years later she was successfully freelancing for national magazines and teaching writing classes herself. She currently teaches writing at the University of Washington's Experimental College and other locations throughout Seattle.

James Thomas Dulley

James Thomas Dulley began writing the weekly Q&A "Cut Your Utility Bills" column four years ago. His column now appears in more than 100 newspapers from California to Maine. His formal education includes a Bachelor of Science in engineering, a Masters of Business in marketing, and doctoral study in the management of technology at the Harvard Business School.

Scott Edelstein

Scott Edelstein has worked as a newspaper, magazine, and book editor. He has written two books for writers: *The No-Experience-Necessary Writer's Course* (Stein and Day, Spring 1987) and *The Indispensable Writer's Guide* (Harper & Row, Fall 1987). His other books include *College: A User's Manual* (Bantam), *Future Pastimes* (Sherbourne Press), and *How to Survive Freshman Composition—and Earn a Higher Grade* (Lyle Stuart, Fall 1988). He has published eighty articles and stories in national magazines; he writes a monthly column, "Question Mark," for *Writer's Digest,* as well as a regular feature for *The Artist's Magazine.*

Patricia Ann Emme

Patricia Ann Emme has been freelance writing for thirty years, working for all the major greeting card companies, such as American Greetings, Gibson, and Rust Craft. She has also sold poetry, articles, and short stories to various national magazines and some of her poetry has been set to music for Christians to sing during their church services.

John D. Engle, Jr.

John D. Engle, Jr. has published more than two thousand poems in various publications, including *The Saturday Evening Post, Good Housekeeping, The Ladies' Home Journal, Commonweal, Writer's Digest,* and *Poem,* as well as numerous anthologies. He has published five books of poetry, a collection of poems and essays, and a one-act play.

Jean Fredette

Jean Fredette was editor of *Fiction Writer's Market* for its first six editions. She also assisted editor Jud Jerome in the first edition of *Poet's Market.* As freelancer she has published in *Writer's Digest, Writer's Yearbook, Cincinnati* Magazine, and local and international publications. Currently she is acquisitions editor of the writing books for Writer's Digest Books.

Dennis E. Hensley

Dennis E. Hensley, Ph.D., is a Writer's Digest regional correspondent and the author of more than 1,500 articles in such periodicals as *Success!, Reader's Digest, Modern Bride, The ABA Journal,* and *Essence.* His fifteen books include *The Competitive Writer's Handbook* (Harper & Row), *Positive Workaholism* (Bobbs-Merrill), *Writing for Profit* (Thomas Nelson), *The Freelancer* (Poetica Press), and with Rose Adkins *Writing for Religious and Other Specialty Markets* (Broadman Publishers). Under the pen name of Leslie Holden, Hensley and Holly G. Miller have written the romance novels *The Legacy of Lillian Parker* and *The Compton Connection.*

Helen Hinckley Jones

Helen Hinckley Jones's fiction and nonfiction has been published by Harpers, Vanguard Lippincott, Ginn and Children's Press. Her books have also been published in Canada and England and have been translated into Dutch, Urdu, Turkish and Swahili.

She is also a successful teacher whose students and former students have published more than seven hundred books with top publishing companies.

Judy Keene

Judy Keene's freelancing started in 1966, when she began selling "about one article every year" to a regional magazine based in Indiana, her home state. The pace soon increased, however, and since that time more than 300 of her articles have appeared in publications as diverse as *The Elks Magazine, Beauty Digest, The Rural Kentuckian,* and the *Princeton Alumni Weekly.* In May 1987, her third book, a collaboration with Indianapolis Mayor William Hudnut entitled *Minister/Mayor,* will be published by The Westminster Press. She currently serves as editor of *Indianapolis Woman,* a monthly magazine.

Peg Kehret

Peg Kehret's plays have been produced in all fifty states and Canada; nineteen of them are published.

Cemeteries Are a Grave Matter, The Divorce Party, and *Charming Billy* are high school favorites. *Let Him Sleep 'till it's Time for His Funeral, Dracula, Darling,* and *Bicycles Built For Two* (a musical) are popular with all ages.

Spirit! won the Forest Roberts Playwriting Award from Northern Michigan University, "Best New Play" from Pioneer Drama Service, and is on the American Theatre Association's list of Best Plays For Senior Adults.

Ms. Kehret's credits also include nonfiction books, juvenile novels, and hundreds of magazine pieces.

Leonard L. Knott

Leonard L. Knott has been writing and getting published for almost sixty-five years. He sold his first article to a national magazine in 1924, and has had three books published in the 80s. A former journalist, public relations consultant, magazine writer and editor, and public speaker, he now teaches creative writing for senior adults. His recent books include *Writing for the Joy of It* and *Writing After Fifty,* from which the excerpt in this volume was taken. Mr. Knott lives in Montreal, Canada, and has one hobby—writing for publication.

Mansfield Latimer

Mansfield Latimer is a retired businessman who now devotes his time to writing, travel, and playing in senior tennis tournaments throughout the country.

Formerly a professional public speaker and newspaper-column writer, Mr. Latimer also established a flower magazine, which had national and international circulation. He writes articles, fiction, and poetry, and sells ideas to cartoonists. His fourth book is scheduled for publication in the spring of 1987.

Don McKinney

Over the past thirty one years, Don McKinney has worked on the staff of three very different magazines: *True, The Man's Magazine, The Saturday Evening Post,* and for the past seventeen years, *McCall's,* where he served as Managing Editor. Before and during that time, he has written dozens of articles on writing, travel, and other subjects, plus mystery stories, short fiction, and thousands of comic books. He is currently a professor at the University of South Carolina, where he teaches magazine writing and the literature of journalism.

John McCollister

Dr. John McCollister, author of eight published books and hundreds of articles in national magazines, earned a B.A. from Capital University, an M. Div. from Trinity Lutheran Seminary, and a Ph.D. from Michigan State University. He has served as a parish pastor, university professor, federal arbitrator, and instructor for the Writer's Digest School. For his active community involvement, he was awarded the "Outstanding American Award" by the Daytona Beach Jaycees. In 1982, he was chosen to give the Lincoln Day Address in Washington, D.C.

Maxine Rock

Maxine Rock is the author of 1,000 magazine articles, which appear in publications such as *Atlanta, Business Atlanta, The South, Southern Accents, Mc-*

Call's, Reader's Digest, Woman's Day, Redbook, Travel & Leisure, Smithsonian, the *New York Times, Die Zeit,* and *Paris and Vie.*

Her books include *Gut Reactions: How to Handle Stress and Your Stomach,* co-authored with Dr. David Taylor; *Fiction Writer's Help Book;* and *The Marriage Map,* which was featured on network and regional TV shows.

Candy Schulman

Candy Schulman's error-free manuscripts have been published in the *New York Times, Glamour, Travel & Leisure, New York Magazine, Writer's Digest,* and other publications. She teaches nonfiction writing workshops at The New School in New York City.

Emalene Shepherd

Emalene Shepherd, an editorial associate of Writer's Digest School, has sold articles to the *New York Times, Today's Christian Woman, Sunday Digest, American Girl, Seek, The Upper Room, Christian Herald, Home Life, Moody Monthly, New World Outlook, Good News, Albuquerque Singles Scene Magazine, Solo,* and other publications. Her main interest is inspirational/personal-experience articles, but her published credits include poetry, a book on writing for teenagers, and a weekly humorous newspaper column, *Pure Fluff.*

Pat Sobleskie

Pat Sobleskie teaches writing through a correspondence course to insurance personnel throughout the U.S. and Canada. Her freelance work has appeared in *Daily Guideposts, 1981, Woman's World, Complete Woman, Ford Times,* and *Grit.*

When not writing professionally, she enjoys volunteer writing for her church's monthly newsletter, and for the local high school band booster club.

William Sunners

William Sunners worked in several printing establishments in various capacities from typesetter to proofreader, then taught graphic arts. Between 1950 and 1981, he wrote a dozen books about winning prizes and creating puzzles of all types. Mr. Sunners has been featured on radio and television programs, including *Late Night with David Letterman,* on numerous occasions.

Royalties from his books enabled him to tour Europe three summers between 1956 and 1973. He is retired and is currently writing *All About Crosswords,* a comprehensive book on the subject.

Carl Wells and Barry Gantt

Carl Wells has written gags for cartoons that have appeared in *Cosmopolitan,* the *Wall Street Journal, Saturday Review,* and other magazines and newspapers. He also taps out humor pieces on his trusty word processor. Barry Gantt is an Oakland, California-based freelance humor writer who has written gags for cartoons that have appeared in *Playboy, The New Yorker,* and many other American magazines. He also serves on the Board of Directors of the Cartoon Art Museum in San Francisco, California.

John Wood

John Wood, a senior editor at *Modern Maturity,* writes three columns for the magazine's 21 million readers each issue. He has also written and photographed for *Basketball Digest, Off Duty, Dynamic Years, Oui* and other magazines. He is currently working on his first novel and reading his first James Michener book—and wondering what took him so long in both cases.

About the Editor

Kirk Polking, a former editor of *Writer's Digest* magazine, is Director of The Writer's Digest School, heading a staff of fifty professional writer/instructors. She is also an experienced freelance writer whose publishing credits include numerous magazine articles and books for both adults and young people, the latest of which are *Oceans of the World: Our Essential Resource* (Philomel Books) and *The Private Pilot's Dictionary and Handbook* (Arco Publishing). In addition, she has edited *Freelance Jobs for Writers, Beginning Writer's Answer Book, Law & the Writer,* and *Writer's Encyclopedia,* all published by Writer's Digest Books.

Index

OTHER BOOKS IN THE
WRITER'S BASIC BOOKSHELF
SERIES

How to Bulletproof Your Manuscript, by Bruce B. Henderson, $9.95

How to Understand & Negotiate a Book Contract or Magazine Agreement, by Richard Balkin, $11.95

How to Write a Book Proposal, by Michael Larsen, $9.95

How to Write Irresistible Query Letters, by Lisa Collier Cool, $10.95

Literary Agents: How to Get & Work with the Right One for You, by Michael Larsen, $9.95

Professional Etiquette for Writers, by William Brohaugh, $9.95

The 29 Most Common Writing Mistakes & How to Avoid Them, by Judy Delton, $9.95

A Writer's Guide to Research, by Lois Horowitz, $9.95

(For a complete catalog of Writer's Digest Books, write to the address below or call TOLL-FREE 1-800-543-4644, outside Ohio.)

To order directly from the publisher, include $2.00 postage and handling for one book, 50¢ for each additional book. Allow 30 days for delivery. Send to:

Writer's Digest Books
1507 Dana Avenue
Cincinnati, OH 45207

Prices subject to change without notice.